"Buy a copy of this book and chain it in the executive washroom."
—*The Dallas Times Herald*

". . . *Refreshing and often entertaining.* . . . *What holds this book together is Ackoff's insight and candor, and his ability to express in one paragraph observations that might require several pages from a less accomplished communicator.*"
—*Sloan Management Review*

"[Ackoff] takes on all comers."
—*The Philadelphia Inquirer*

". . . *Ackoff's book is full of common sense. He substitutes management by thinking for management by wandering around.* . . . *Ackoff excels at turning problems upside down to reveal hidden solutions.*"
—*Across The Board*

". . . 52 subjects of vital interest to all who participate in the management of an organization. Each can be read in two or three minutes—each deserves to be thought about for two or three hours."
—Sanford N. McDonnell, Chairman and CEO
McDonnell Douglas

". . . *A gem—a fast trip through a lot of important and crucial leadership and management issues—a fast trip, but a profitable and rewarding experience.*"
—Robert H. Gaynor, Vice President
AT&T Communications

"A very, very bright man with a genuine sense of humor and an intense curiosity . . . a reading of Management in Small Doses *will reveal these characteristics of the man.*"
—Thomas G. Pownall, Chairman and CEO
Martin Marietta Corporation

". . . *Contains marvelous nuggets of management information which should be of benefit to managers at all levels.*"
—Sam S. McKeel, President
Philadelphia Newspapers, Inc.

MANAGEMENT IN SMALL DOSES

RUSSELL L. ACKOFF
The Wharton School
University of Pennsylvania
Philadelphia, Pennsylvania

JOHN WILEY & SONS
New York / Chichester / Brisbane / Toronto / Singapore

Published by John Wiley & Sons, Inc.
All rights reserved. Published simultaneously in Canada.

Library of Congress Cataloging in Publication Data:

Ackoff, Russell Lincoln, 1919-
    Management in small doses.

    1. Management.   3   I. Title.
HD31.A283 1986   658   86-7835
ISBN 0-471-84822-0
ISBN 0-471-61765-2 (paperback)

Printed in the United States of America

10 9 8 7

To

Jim Rinehart

who manages
to educate
as well as
manage

Foreword

"Management in Small Doses" by Russ Ackoff is an absolute delight. Here are 52 sparkling and provocative essays on management topics, each one easily read in three or four minutes. The author recommends one per week, so he gives us a full year's supply. Few will follow his prescription. I found myself gobbling them down in much more substantial dosages.

Ackoff writes with a marvelous wit and practical common sense that will appeal to the business reader. He is highly irreverent, a smasher of so-called "accepted wisdom," yet never irrelevant nor given to rhetorical hyperbole. Just read his essay on business jargon to understand this point. This is no huckster, but rather a respected academic who has honed his skills in the real world of business. How else could he write an essay on "Mess Management" in which he says, "We do not experience individual problems, but complex systems of strongly interacting problems. I like to call them messes." You and I know these are the situations we face in our businesses.

Don't miss his essay on "Advertising: Wonder or Waste." Here are insights and examples that are worth the price of the book, besides providing some real chuckles.

After delving into these essays you may agree with the author's statement, "business schools do a much better job of educating their faculty than their students." At least here's one very well educated faculty member.

REGINALD H. JONES

Retired Chairman and CEO,
General Electric Company

Preface

In the autumn of 1984 Dean Russell Palmer of The Wharton School asked me if I would do a commentary on an about-to-be-launched weekly cable television program, *Management Report*. I agreed, with reservations.

First, my usual presentations consist of one- to three-hour lectures. To say something worthwhile in no more than the four minutes allotted to me seemed virtually impossible.

Second, television's primary function is to entertain, but I am an educator, not an entertainer. Moreover, I am an educator who depends critically on feedback from a live audience. I knew I could not entertain, and I doubted that I could even educate, when addressing a camera and its operator, who is concealed behind the camera, in an otherwise empty studio.

Despite my doubts and deficiencies, Chris Graves, the program's producer, and Alice Priest, its editor, worked long and hard on and with me. They even tried to act as an audience. I survived about 30 telecasts, after which the program was discontinued for lack of financial support.

Although most of my commentaries were delivered without a script, I worked out my thoughts on paper beforehand. I showed a sample of them to my old friend and collaborator C. West Churchman. He told me that they made better reading than listening and suggested their publication. Therefore, he is to blame for this.

After *Management Report* was taken off the air I continued to prepare scripts because I had grown fond of trying to express an idea succinctly. About 20 of these "posthumous" commentaries are included in this work. Although each script was prepared as an independent entity, I have tried to order them to give some semblance of continuity.

Because it is my hope that these commentaries will be discussed and played with intellectually, the recommended dosage is one per week. If my recommendation is followed, this book will provide a year's supply.

The commentaries are intended to provoke thought and discussion, not necessarily to evoke agreement. I have no desire to think *for* managers, but I do enjoy thinking *with* and *about* them, particularly with and about those who think for themselves.

I have received a great deal of constructive criticism and encouragement from Tom Cowan, who has been doing this to me for about 45 years. He has taught me a lot more than I know. I am also grateful to Professor Harvey Hornstein for his helpful suggestions.

RUSSELL L. ACKOFF

Philadelphia, Pennsylvania
June 1986

Contents

MANAGEMENT IN SMALL DOSES

1

Profit

Profit is necessary for the survival of a business enterprise but not the reason for it. Profit is a requirement, not an objective; a means, not an end. The American humorist Ambrose Bierce put this clearly when he defined money as "a blessing that is of no advantage to us excepting when we part with it."

Efforts to maximize profit are efforts to obtain money to use for something else. What should this something else be? *Growth?* No. Growth is also a means, not an end. This is apparent when we consider how undesirable growth is when it is accompanied by reduced profit. Growth may, of course, increase profit. But what should profit be used for and why growth?

The objectives pursued by organizations frequently differ from those proclaimed. I learned this from spending 45 years in universities. Like many, when I started I assumed that the principal objective of universities was the education of students. Armed with this assumption, I could make no sense of their behavior. I learned that education of students, like profit, is at most a requirement of universities, not an objective. I also learned that *their principal objective is to provide their faculties with the quality of work life and standard of living they desire.* This enabled me to understand why professors do so little teaching, give the same courses over and over again, arrange classes at their own convenience, not that of their students, teach subjects they want to teach rather than those the students want to learn, give examinations that are easy to grade rather than facilitate learning, and skip classes to give lectures for a fee.

Universities are not unique in this regard. Corporations are much the same. Having worked in several hundred of them, I am convinced that those who manage them do so primarily to provide themselves with the quality of work life and standard of living they desire. I believe their behavior can be better understood by assuming this than by assuming that their objective is to maximize profit or growth.

I see no reason to apologize for this objective. The only thing wrong with it is its coverage. It should be extended to cover the quality of work life and standard of living of *all* employees. This quality and standard cannot be improved without making a profit, without paying dividends large enough to attract and retain investors, without increasing productivity so as to be competitive, and without growth to absorb those employees displaced by increased productivity.

The termination of an enterprise has a greater effect on its employees than on any of its other stakeholders—the lower their level, the greater their stake. Employees have the greatest stake and make the largest investment in their employing organization and incur the greatest losses when it goes out of business.

To provide employees at every level with work that is interesting and financially rewarding and that provides opportunities for personal development is something to be proud of, not to apologize for or conceal. It can also give a company's shareholders and the community of which it is a part something to be proud of. It can even help sales. Volvo, for one, has found this to be the case.

It is time for corporate executives to stop pretending they are not caring people and to start enlarging the number of people for whom they care.

REFLECTIONS*

_____

_____

_____

*My hope is that each piece in this book provokes thought about the way things are done in your organization. So, at the end of each piece you'll find a brief space to record your reflections. You may find it a handy place to jot down your ideas.

2

Consumer Design

Producers often try to find out what consumers want by asking them. This seldom yields useful information because consumers either don't know what they want or they try to provide (or avoid) answers they think are expected of them. In many cases a better way consists of using the consumer to *design* products or services; for example, a chain of men's stores, although successful, failed to attract the type of customer its owner wanted. He wanted to reach upwardly mobile professionals and businessmen by offering high-quality designer clothing at discount prices. But this method failed; rather it drew bargain hunters from lower income segments of the population. Repeated questionnaires addressed to potential buyers the firm wanted to attract yielded results that, when applied, failed to bring them into the stores.

The owner and his executives sought help from a research group with a reputation for unconventional approaches to marketing problems. This group selected 15 representatives of the targeted customer population and invited them to spend a Saturday designing their ideal men's store. The identity of the sponsoring firm was not revealed but several of its executives took part incognito.

The representatives of the targeted population produced a very creative design of a men's store. Once done, the identity of the sponsor was revealed and a comparison was made of the sponsor's stores with the one newly designed. The principal differences were wide and had not been revealed by any of the earlier research.

Here are a few of the differences. First, the designers made it known that they always decided how much to spend for articles of clothing before shopping. What they were looking for was a store that offered the highest quality at their predetermined price. Put another way: they did *not* want to minimize price for a predetermined quality; they wanted to *maximize quality* for a predetermined price. Discount prices, the chain's advertising message, turned them off.

Second, they wanted different articles of clothing of the same size to be segregated. They did not want grouping by type, which requires hunting all around the store.

Third, they wanted to examine clothing without a salesman hovering over them. They wanted call buttons installed in each size-organized area for summoning a salesman when *they* wanted one.

Fourth, they did not want items for women in the store—not even gifts. They preferred to shop for women in stores that specialize in products suitable to them, just as they preferred to buy their own clothing in stores that specialize in supplying men. But they did want a lounge in which women could pass their time pleasantly and comfortably and be available for consultation. They thought a mixture of male and female salespersons would be desirable.

They wanted alteration costs included in the price of the clothing and delivery of all altered clothing. They also wanted more informative labels with complete information on the material used, where the clothing was made, and by whom. They said they were uninterested in the designer's name; they didn't believe that the designer identified on men's clothing had designed it anyhow.

As regular customers of a store they wanted access to its sales before the general public. They thought that there should be only two sales a year, presummer and prewinter, to occur at the same time each year. They also wanted the store to maintain and refer to records of their sizes and style preferences.

Similar consumer design groups have been used for other types of product and service, and even to write advertising copy. They have always been creative and informative.

It is harder for a market researcher to get inside a consumer's mind than it is for a consumer to turn his mind inside out.

REFLECTIONS

_____

_____

_____

_____

3

Appropriate Technology

As labor-intensive industries migrate from more to less developed countries (from MDCs to LDCs) the LDCs need easy-to-maintain production equipment that is appropriate to labor-intensive processes. Most of the production equipment currently available to LDCs is inappropriate because it was designed for use in MDCs. Equipment used in LDCs should be designed with *their* costs of labor, energy, and capital in mind, not those of MDCs; for example, old and new trucks designed in MDCs incorporate an assumed economic value of the drivers' lives. This assumption determines how much safety is designed into trucks. The life of a driver cannot be assumed to be infinitely valuable because an infinite amount of money cannot be spent to protect it. The maximum average amount that a society can spend to protect the lives of its members cannot exceed the present value of their expected net contribution to their society's wealth over their lives. This amount obviously varies from society to society; it is proportional to the wealth of countries. Therefore, a truck designed with safety features appropriate to an MDC is considerably overdesigned for use in an LDC. This is equally true for most manufacturing equipment.

Furthermore, the appropriateness of equipment depends on climatic, regulatory, and cultural, as well as economic, conditions.

Markets in LDCs may not be large enough now to justify the design and production of some types of equipment appropriate to them. In many such cases compromises are possible; for example, trucks and production equipment currently produced in MDCs often can be modified and stripped down to make them more appropriate to LDCs.

New factories are being built in rural areas of LDCs to alleviate overcrowded conditions in their major cities and to promote rural development. Factories that are appropriate in cities in MDCs are not appropriate in rural areas of LDCs. Rural factories could be designed to serve as water-pumping and electricity-generating stations even if they performed these functions only during off-hours. Material-handling equipment could be designed to be useful on farms when not in use in factories.

Mobile facilities are particularly appropriate in many LDCs. In Mexico, for example, CONASUPO uses mobile markets to provide food for small, remote rural communities. There is no reason why factories cannot also be made mobile. Mobile food-processing plants, that move from place to place as sequentially planned crops become ready for processing, might be useful in some LDCs. One chemical company in an MDC has built a factory on a barge which they tow to different ports as needed and a factory that manufactures houses has been built into a set of truck trailers for transportation from one construction site to another.

Many consumer products supplied to LDCs by MDCs are also inappropriate. Even when these products are manufactured in LDCs they usually retain designs that are not totally suitable. Western clothing is an example. This clothing, which is often not functional even in MDCs, is seldom as functional in LDCs as native dress. Yet as many LDCs develop they adopt Western dress because it is taken as a symbol of development.

The same is true of automobiles. Most cars designed in MDCs are inappropriate in LDCs. Their cost is excessive because they have properties of little or no value to LDCs; for example, studies done in Mexico City show that the average number of occupants in automobiles, including taxis, is 1.2. Less than 15 percent of the cars carry more than two people, which suggests that a two-passenger vehicle would serve LDCs better even than the "small" four-passenger vehicles produced in MDCs. Two-passenger automobiles sensibly designed for urban use in LDCs would cost no more than half as much as the least expensive automobile currently available in MDCs. This cost could be reduced further by designing automobiles that could be assembled by purchasers.

Use of small urban automobiles would considerably reduce traffic congestion, air pollution, and energy consumption, which are critical problems in many LDCs. Research has shown that if these vehicles were designed to
seat the passenger behind (not beside) the driver, and
they were used exclusively, 2.2 times as many people
could be carried on expressways and 2.7 to 5.4 times as
many on city streets, depending on parking arrangements.

By developing equipment, facilities, and products appropriate to LDCs, companies in MDCs could not only create
new business opportunities but could contribute
significantly to the development of the less developed
countries of the world.

REFLECTIONS

_____

_____

_____

_____

4

Acquisitions

A great deal has been written about how to make a successful acquisition and much of it is useful. Despite this, however, some aspects of making an acquisition appear to me to receive too little attention in practice.

More attention is usually given to what the acquired company can contribute to the acquiring company than the other way around. The premiums required to make most acquisitions should be justified by potential additions to the value of the company acquired. Put another way: the principal question should not be "What can the acquisition candidate do for us?" but "What can we do for it?" A corporation that consists of more than one business cannot be justified unless the whole is worth more than the sum of its parts. Therefore, unless the acquiring company can add value to the company to be acquired, the acquisition should not take place.

More than the usual amount of attention should be given to the quality of the candidate's facilities and equipment. These assets should be thoroughly examined by competent members of the acquiring firm. If they are below that firm's standards, estimates should be made of the cost of "elevating" them. This cost is frequently overlooked or underestimated.

However attractive an acquisition candidate may appear, acquiring it is likely to succeed only if the managers of the two companies like, respect, and trust one another. To find out whether they do, they should interact in and out of the business environment as much as possible before the acquisition is made.

Despite all precautions, once an acquisition is made the acquiring company may find it necessary to manage and operate the acquired company. Are the technologies, skills, and knowledge required to do so available in the acquiring company? If not, the candidate should not be considered.

More attention is usually given to an acquisition candidate's past performance than to its potential. The value of an acquired company lies in its future, not its past. Therefore, a company contemplating an acquisition should make itself thoroughly familiar with, and carefully evaluate, the candidate's strategy for coping with its competitive environment and the dynamics of this environment. If management of the acquiring company is not capable of evaluating that strategy, or fixing it if necessary, the acquisition should not be made.

Does the possibility of entering the acquisition candidate's business excite and present a challenge to the management of the acquiring company? Will involvement in its business be a source of pride and fun? Has it conducted its business ethically and been socially responsible? Are its employment practices compatible with those of the acquiring firm? How do the candidate's employees at all levels feel about their employer and the acquiring firm?

I have found that most acquiring companies do not know enough about acquisition candidates to answer these questions. They seldom identify or speak to former employees of the candidate, nor do they consult its suppliers, customers, security analysts, and bankers. Too low a value is placed on comprehensive "intelligence."

The best way I know to learn about a candidate before acquiring it is to set up a joint task force, which would consist of managers of both companies, to prepare a detailed plan for the integration of the acquired company into the one acquiring it. This, of course, can be done only when the acquisition is "friendly." An "unfriendly" acquisition usually precludes the possibility of getting enough information about the candidate to make good decisions.

Acquisition of a company is like adopting a child. How that child develops depends on its genes as well as on the adopting parents. One cannot learn too much about the genetic characteristics of an adopted child or company.

To use another metaphor: the management of a company in search of an acquisition should think of itself as piloting a plane about to take off. It should not rely on its memory to do all the right things in the right order. It should have a checklist of things to be done and know what to do if any of its actions fail to bring about the expected result. In particular, it should know when to abort the takeoff.

REFLECTIONS

_____

_____

_____

_____

5

The Corporation Reconceived

The Industrial Revolution took place in the United States in the last century. As industrial enterprises grew in size and number a conceptual model was needed. Not surprisingly, the concept that emerged corresponded to the prevailing concept of the world. Following Newton, the world was conceptualized as a machine created by God to do His work; the function of man, as part of that machine, was to serve God's purposes. Therefore, industrial enterprises were first thought of as machines created by their "gods," the owners, to serve their purpose in creating these enterprises, which was to make a profit. An enterprise was seen as having no purpose of its own but as serving that of its owner. Within an enterprise the owner was a virtual god, with almost limitless power, subject to almost no externally imposed constraints. Like a machine, the ideal enterprise was one that could operate independently of its environment.

Workers were viewed and treated as replaceable machine parts. This treatment was possible because (1) workers had virtually no source of income other than employment, (2) they were poorly educated and had low levels of aspiration, (3) few skills were required, and (4) replacements were plentiful.

By World War I social and economic development required a change in the concept of an enterprise. If enterprises were to take advantage of the opportunities for growth that had become available to them, they required external financing. Owners had to choose between retaining complete control and restricting growth, and sharing ownership to obtain the resources required to grow as rapidly as possible. Many chose to share ownership and "went public." "God" disappeared, was dispersed, and became an abstract spirit. As had occurred when the God of the Western World disappeared 20 centuries earlier, a clergy—management—was created to serve as an intermediary between the workers and "god." The managers knew the will of the owners as the clergy knew that of God, by revelation, and transmitted it to the workers.

Meanwhile the workers had become more educated, had the beginnings of social security, were increasingly protected by unions, and were more difficult to replace because of the greater skills required of them. They could no longer be treated as replaceable machine parts.

These conditions led to the reconceptualization of the business enterprise as a *corporation*—derived from *corpus*, body—therefore, as an *organism*. Like all organisms, corporations had an overriding purpose of their own, *survival*, for which *growth* was taken to be essential. As Peter Drucker said, profit came to be viewed as oxygen is for a human being: necessary for its survival but not the reason for it. The CEO became the *head* of the firm and management, its *brain*. Departments were thought of much as bodily organs and workers, as cells. Their health and safety became major concerns that were reflected in labor legislation and contracts. The environment was viewed as a purposeless self-renewing source of resources and a receptacle for waste.

World War II and a permissively raised generation of well-educated and socially secure workers changed all this. Government and such special interest groups as ecologists and consumer advocates began to demand *responsible* behavior from corporations. Well-educated workers, increasingly alienated by the machinelike labor required of them, began to demand more satisfying and challenging work and opportunities for personal development.

As a result, industrial enterprises are once again being reconceptualized, this time as *social systems*. An enterprise viewed as a social system is considered (1) to be a part of a larger social system (society) that has purposes of its own and (2) to contain individuals who have purposes of their own. The purpose of an enterprise is apparently becoming one of serving the needs and desires of all its stakeholders, not the stockholders alone. Survival and growth are increasingly becoming a means to this end, not ends in themselves. When an enterprise increases its ability and its desire to serve its stakeholders, it *develops*. *Development* is more and more commonly taken to be the appropriate purpose of an enterprise.

This social-systemic, service-oriented view of a corporation is completely different from the organismic view of it as an entity served by passive environments and stakeholders. Today, employees, including managers, are increasingly believed to have the largest investment in firms and therefore, to be their most important stakeholders. From society's point of view corporations are instruments for *producing and distributing wealth*, primarily by employment. Therefore, the provision of jobs is perceived as one of their major social responsibilities.

Of what significance is this evolution of the conception of industrial enterprises? It is this: *in a society that views and treats corporations as social systems, as instruments for serving their stakeholders' interests, corporations that are managed as though they were machines or organisms are not likely to survive and grow.*

REFLECTIONS

_____

_____

_____

_____

6

Mess Management

Problems are to reality what atoms are to tables. We experience tables, not atoms. Problems are abstracted from experience by analysis. We do not experience individual problems but complex systems of those that are strongly interacting. I call them *messes*.

Suboptimization may not be the best thing.

Because *messes* are *systems* of problems, they lose their essential properties when they are taken apart. Therefore, if a mess is disassembled, it loses its essential properties. Furthermore, as in any system, if each part taken separately is treated as well as possible, the whole is *not* treated as well as possible. A system is more than the sum of its parts; it is the product of their interactions. If taken apart, it simply disappears. Then how can we formulate a mess without taking it apart?

It can be done by the use of *reference projections.* These are projections of the performance of an enterprise that are based on two *false* assumptions. First, it is assumed that the organization involved will not change any of its current plans, policies, or practices. If this were true, the organization would not be trying to formulate its mess. Second, it is assumed that the organization's environment will change only as expected; this is obviously false. Under these assumptions the performance of the organization is projected into the future. These projections reveal the future implied by the organization's current plans, policies, and practices: *the future it is in.*

No matter how successful an organization is, reference projections taken collectively reveal how it would destroy itself if it were not to change. These projections reveal the Achilles heel of the organization. They do this because the no-change assumption implies no adaptation even to a predictably changing environment; for example, projections were made in 1959 which revealed the impending crisis of the American automotive industry. By using data from the preceding 40 years projections were made of (1) the number of people of driving age in the United States in the year 2000, (2) the number of cars per person of driving age, (3) the number of miles driven per car per year, and (4) the percentage of these miles driven within cities. By combining these projections an estimate was prepared of the number of urban automobile miles that would be driven in the United States in the year 2000 if the industry continued on its then current path and its environment changed only as expected.

Next, by using these projections an estimate was made of

the additional parking space and lane-miles of streets and highways that would be needed in the year 2000 to maintain 1960 levels of congestion. Then the cost of their construction, estimated by using projected construction costs, revealed that more than 12 times the maximum amount ever spent per year in the United States for such construction would be required for each of the next 40 years. Although these expenditures were unlikely, they were, in fact, implicitly assumed in the plans then in force in the industry.

This was not the mess facing the industry, however. The mess was revealed by assuming that these large expenditures would be made. If they were, 117 percent of the surfaces of American cities would be covered by streets, highways, and parking lots by the year 2000. This, of course, could not happen. Therefore, continued growth of the automotive industry as it had been was not possible. This was the mess.

What would prevent cities from being covered by streets, highways, and parking lots? The answer rested in decisions still to be made. Studies showed that one way to avoid the mess would be to reduce the size of automobiles. The American automotive industry chose not to do so at that time. It waited for more than a decade before the cost of oil, foreign competition, and government requirements forced it to move slightly in that direction. The consequences of the industry's failure to pay attention to its mess are well known.

We have to know where we are headed before we can take action to avoid getting there. Such redirection of an enterprise requires *mess management,* not problem solving, and mess management requires creative and comprehensive planning.

REFLECTIONS

Reference Projection can project what will happen if expected environmental changes come true and if the mgmt. operate under its policy, plan, etc w/o changes to adapt to the environment. From there mgmt. can see what might happen and what problems might be encountered. Then mgmt. can redirect the organization in a better direction.

7

Growth Versus Development

Growth and development are not the same thing. Neither is necessary for the other. A rubbish heap can grow but it doesn't develop. Artists can develop without growing. Nevertheless, many managers take development to be the same as growth. Most efforts directed at corporate development are actually directed at corporate growth.

To grow is to increase in size or number. *To develop is to increase one's ability and desire to satisfy one's own needs and legitimate desires and those of others.* A legitimate desire is one that, when satisfied, does not impede the development of anyone else.

Development is an increase in capability and competence.

Development of individuals and corporations is more a matter of learning than earning. It has less to do with how much one has than how much one can do with whatever one has. For this reason Robinson Crusoe is a better model of development than Jean Paul Getty.

Development is better reflected in quality of life than in standard of living. Therefore, the level of development of a corporation is better reflected in the quality of work life it provides its employees than in its profit-and-loss statement.

If an undeveloped country or corporation was flooded with money it would be richer but no more developed. On the other hand, if a well-developed country or corporation was suddenly deprived of wealth, it would not be less developed.

A well-developed country or corporation can do more with its resources than one that is less developed. This is *not* to say that the amount of resources available is irrelevant. Resources can be used to accelerate development and improve quality of life, but they can best be used for these purposes by those who are developed.

Growth and development do not have to conflict; they can reinforce each other. The best evidence that this is happening is a simultaneous increase in standard of living and quality of life. However, there is currently a widespread belief that quality of life is being sacrificed to increase standard of living. This belief is accompanied by a willingness to sacrifice standard of living to improve quality of life, a willingness that is reflected in the environmentalist movement.

A lack of resources can limit growth but not development. The more developed individuals, organizations, or societies becomes the less they depend on resources and the more they can do with whatever resources they have. They also have the ability and the desire to create or acquire the resources they need.

An individual can grow too much. Some people and many societies believe that a corporation can too. *But would anyone argue that individuals, corporations, or countries can develop too much?*

REFLECTIONS

Individuals and organizations should direct more attention on development than growth. The need for growth may change due to situation and external factors can limit growth. There is a constant need for development and external factor can hinder development but not limit development.

8

The Value of a Corporation

What justification can there be for combining two or more businesses in one corporation? The answer is obvious: the corporation adds value to its parts or, put another way, the value of the corporation taken as a whole is greater than the sum of the values of its parts taken separately. That many corporations do not meet this condition was made apparent in a recent article in *BusinessWeek* (July 8, 1985, pp. 80f):

> Breakup value is the new buzzword on Wall Street. It is a measure of the separate prices that the market would place on the parts of a company. And the new hot stocks are those where the sum of the parts amounts to far more than the current stock price.

The same article identified a number of companies for which a sample of security analysts believed this to be true. Included were such well known corporations as Colgate-Palmolive, General Foods, General Mills, Parker Pen, Ralston Purina, and Revlon.

A corporation can add to the value of its separate businesses in a number of ways, of which the following is only a small sample.

First, it can provide synergy, that is, opportunities for two or more businesses to cooperate in ways that would not be possible if they were separate; for example, economies of scale and increases in effectiveness can be obtained by sharing legal services, research and development, education and training, purchasing, distribution, and marketing. A corporation may also combine the products of different businesses into marketable systems.

Second, a corporation can often provide its parts with more capital at a lower cost than they could obtain if they were separate businesses.

Third, corporate management can provide guidance that improves the management of its business units.

Fourth, a corporation may be able to exert greater favorable influence over the political and social environment of its individual businesses than they could separately.

One could go on listing the ways in which a corporation can add value to its parts. For each, however, there is a corresponding way in which it can decrease that value; for example, it can impose costly and ineffective services on them, it can deprive them of the capital they would otherwise be able to invest in their own development and growth, and it can reduce the effectiveness of their managements by excessive control from the top.

To avoid decreasing the value of its parts, corporate managers should engage in periodic dialogue with the managers of its parts to determine whether they feel that they would be more valuable if they were operating independently or as part of another corporation. If the management of a part believes this to be the case, the reasons for it should be discussed with corporate management. Steps should be taken to change the views of the part's management or it should be allowed to secede from the union.

Those of us who live in a democracy believe that the right to emigrate is one of the most important its members enjoy. Without it, individuals become instruments of the state. In a democracy the state should be the instrument of its members. When individuals no longer feel that the state or the part of which they are members is adequately serving their interests, they should have the right to move to another part or emigrate from the whole. The right to emigrate, to quit, is given to employees of corporations, but in many their ability to move between parts is very much constrained.

Corporations have the right to emigrate from one country to another, but because a corporation *owns* its parts, these parts lack the right to move to another corporation. Parts of a state are similarly denied the right to withdraw from it because they too are believed to be owned by it. Yet most

Americans believe that Poland, for example, should have the right to secede from the Soviet Union, the Kurds from Iran, or the Basques from Spain. Is this hypocrisy?

Unless parts of a corporate or political union have the right to secede, they can be enslaved, and those who manage or govern the whole can be deprived of the feedback that enables them to evaluate performance effectively. What better and more effective union can there be than one whose parts have chosen to belong to that union?

REFLECTIONS

If the objective of the corporation is to maximize its value then its part should have the right to operate and manage itself independently so as the max. the value of the part. The part of the corporation may be separated only if it can operate more efficiently and it will increase its value. People judge the value of a corporation by adding its parts up as if each part is an independent business. So to max. corporation value is to max. value of each business as if they were operating independently.

9

The Economy of the Firm

A curious contradiction is present in the ways we run our national macroeconomy and the microeconomies of the business enterprises within it. At the national level we favor a market economy that is regulated as little as is compatible with national interests. The economies of most of our business enterprises, however, are run much like the national economy of the Soviet Union. They are centrally planned and controlled, transfer pricing is imposed on the parts, and when internal sources of products or services are available they are usually run as bureaucratic monopolies.

What would a corporation look like if it were run like the American economy?

Each component would be a profit center *free* to buy and sell products and services wherever it wanted to—free, but subject to *as little regulation* by corporate management as required for the good of the whole. Corporate management would have the function of government within the firm. Moreover, each unit would have to pay corporately imposed taxes on its profits, interest, or dividends on the capital obtained from the corporation, and, unless the corporation believed in free trade, duties on some imports to, and exports from, the corporation.

Only a few corporations approximate this way of operating. Why?

Two reasons are usually given. First, centralized planning and control are said to maximize synergy between the parts of a corporation. But there is no lack of synergy between suppliers, producers, and consumers in the national economy. Many corporate producers experience less conflict and more cooperation with external suppliers and customers than with those that are internal.

Second, it is argued that some economies of scale enjoyed by corporations would be lost in a "free corporate economy"; but such losses are not necessary. Parts of a corporation can form buying, producing, and selling cooperatives just as independent enterprises do in the national economy. This cooperation can be encouraged by corporate management, just as it is by governments of most free national economies.

Moreover, a market economy within the firm can avoid some diseconomies of scale. Large internal monopolies are often no more efficient than those that are external and tend to be less sensitive and responsive to their customers than smaller internal units that must compete with external suppliers for internal business.

It is possible for corporate management to intervene in the transactions of the units reporting to it as our government can but seldom does. Suppose headquarters wants one internal unit to buy from another internal unit but the buying unit does not want to because the internal supplier demands a higher price than an external source. Corporate management can pay the buying unit the difference. Unless it did, the buying unit would be free to use an external source. This requirement would discourage corporate management from arbitrarily restraining external trade. It would have to pay for these restraints and therefore would not be likely to impose them unless it believed the corporation as a whole would benefit.

In a corporate market economy corporate headquarters would receive income from taxes on unit profits, import and export duties, and interest or dividends from units for funds it provided. It would pay for any profit-reducing constraints it imposed on internal units and for any services it obtained from them. This would make it possible for the headquarters itself to be a profit center. Its profits or losses would not be the same as the corporation's. Therefore, the effectiveness of corporate management could be evaluated in the same way as that of business units.

Isn't it time for corporations to practice the same type of economy they preach to the nation?

REFLECTIONS

If corporations are decentralized as to decision making
efficiency make not be lost further efficiency may
be gained.   Corporate mgmt. make be measured
for their performance and how they can help individual
business units achieve their goals in a way that is
also good for the corporation as a whole. Individual
business units gain more freedom to achieve its goals.

10

Performance Measurement

important

Those corporate managers who can't measure what they want frequently settle for wanting what they can measure.

Earnings, return on investment or assets, sales volume, price-earning ratios, cash flow, and market share are among the more commonly used measures of annual corporate performance. The deficiencies of these measures, used separately or in combination, are well known. Nevertheless, they are widely used because better measures do not appear to be available.

Efforts to maximize any measure of annual performance usually sacrifice future performance; for example, one company in the food business paid its regional managers, who were responsible for production and sales, a bonus based on their net profit in the preceding year. These payments were as much as five times their base salaries. To maximize their annual bonuses these managers increased prices and reduced product quality, expenditures on maintenance, and investments in plant modernization. After several years of these practices the company's price spreads became so large and its quality differentials so small that its market shares and volumes suffered significantly. The regional managers could no longer maintain their prices, let alone reduce them to meet competition. Profits went down the drain.

Obviously companies do not want to sacrifice the future for better current performance, but they do not know how to measure their future performance. Therefore, they want what they can measure: last year's performance as conventionally evaluated. There is an alternative.

The current value of a company is reflected, however imperfectly, in the highest price someone is willing to pay to acquire it. One who acquires a company is buying its *future*, not its past. Thus, estimates of the current market value of an enterprise are based on its expected performance, *its potential*. Companies and their units should try to increase this potential and their performance should be measured by changes in it.

A company that invests heavily in its future and pays for it with a reduction in current profits is much to be preferred to one that has allowed its future to deteriorate to increase current profits.

Clearly, a company's performance potential cannot always be estimated accurately. Nevertheless, it *is* estimated by anyone who contemplates acquiring it. Experts are sometimes used to prepare these estimates. Whether done internally or externally, they often turn out to be quite good. Companies can and should use these estimates to evaluate their own and the performances of their parts.

These measures may not be as accurate as those commonly used to evaluate past performance, but *it is better to use imprecise measures of what is wanted than precise measures of what is not.* Is it a question of relevance vs. irrelevancy or past vs. present.

REFLECTIONS

Performance measure should not be based on what's being done for the past or present but for the future. So current profit shouldn't be the only important factor for performance measurement. Emphasis should be on what someone would pay for its potential. What companies want is to increase its expected performance or potential. Whether they know exactly how much potential is increased is not as important because they know what they are aiming for and not aiming at a wrong target to measure performance.

11

Mission
Statements

Most corporate mission statements are worthless. They consist largely of pious platitudes such as: "We will hold ourselves to the highest standards of professionalism and ethical behavior." They often formulate necessities as objectives; for example, "to achieve sufficient profit." This is like a person saying his mission is to breathe sufficiently. A mission statement should not commit a firm to what it *must* do in order to survive but to what it *chooses* to do in order to thrive. Nor should it be filled with operationally meaningless superlatives such as *biggest, best, optimum, and maximum*; for example, one company says it wants to "maximize its growth potential," another "to provide products of the highest quality." How in the world can a company determine whether it has attained its maximum growth potential or highest quality?

To test for the appropriateness of an assertion in a mission statement, determine whether it can be disagreed with reasonably. If not, it should be excluded. Can you imagine any company disagreeing with the objective "to provide the best value for the money." If you can't, it's not worth saying.

What characteristics should a mission statement have? First, *it should contain a formulation of the firm's objectives that enables progress toward them to be measured.* To state objectives that cannot be used to evaluate performance is hypocrisy. Unless the adoption of a mission statement changes the behavior of the firm that makes it, it has no value.

The behavior of a Mexican firm was profoundly affected by the following passage from its mission statement:

> To create a wholesome, varied, pluralistic, multiclass recreational area incorporating tourist facilities and permanent residences, and to produce locally as much of the goods and services required by the area as possible, so as to improve the standard of living and quality of life of its inhabitants.

Second, *a company's mission statement should differentiate it from other companies.* It should establish the individuality, if not the uniqueness, of the firm. A company that wants only what most other companies want—for example, "to manufacture products in an efficient manner, at costs that help yield adequate profits"—wastes its time in formulating a mission statement. Individuality can be attained in many ways, including that in which a company's business is identified.

Third, *a mission statement should define the business that the company wants to be in, not necessarily is in.* However diverse its current businesses, it should try to find a unifying concept that enlarges its view of itself and brings it into focus; for example, a company that produces beverages, snacks, and baked goods and operates a variety of dining, recreational, and entertainment facilities identified its business as "increasing the satisfaction people derive from use of their discretionary time." This suggested completely new directions for its diversification and growth. The same was true of a company that said it was in the "sticking" business, enabling objects and materials to stick together.

Fourth, *a mission statement should be relevant to all the firm's stakeholders.* These include its customers, suppliers, the public, shareholders, and employees. The mission should state how the company intends to serve each of them; for example, one company committed itself "to providing all its employees with adequate and fair compensation, safe working conditions, stable employment, challenging work, opportunities for personal development, and a satisfying quality of working life." It also wanted "to provide those who supply the material used in the business with continuing, if not expanding, sources of business, and with incentives to improve their products and services and their use through research and development."

Most mission statements address only shareholders and managers. Their most serious deficiency is their failure to motivate nonmanagerial employees. Without their commitment, a company's mission has little chance of being fulfilled, whatever its managers and shareholders do.

Finally, and of greatest importance, *a mission statement should be exciting and inspiring*. It should motivate all those whose participation in its pursuit is sought; for example, one Latin American company committed itself to being "an active force for economic and social development, fostering economic integration of Latin America and, within each country, collaboration between government, industry, labor and the public." A mission should play the same role in a company that the Holy Grail did in the Crusades. It does *not* have to appear to be feasible: it only has to be *desirable*:

> . . . man has been able to grow enthusiastic over his vision of . . . unconvincing enterprises. He has put himself to work for the sake of an idea, seeking by magnificent exertions to arrive at the incredible. And in the end he has arrived there. Beyond all doubt it is one of the vital sources of man's power, to be thus able to kindle enthusiasm from the mere glimmer of something improbable, difficult, remote.*

If your firm has a mission statement, test it against these five criteria. If it fails to meet any of them, it should be redone.

---

*José Ortega y Gasset, *Mission of the University*, Norton, New York, 1966, p. 1.

If your firm has no mission statement, one should be prepared and as participatively as possible. An organization
without a *shared vision* of what it wants to be is like a trav-
eler without a destination. It has no way of determining
whether it is making progress.

REFLECTIONS

A mission statement must be meaningful and give the
company a direction where it wants to go. The mission
statement must be measurable in terms of its progress, individualized
and unlike other companies, the business the firm is in or
wants to be in, it must be relevant to all stakeholders,
and it must be inspiring and exciting. The mission
statement is what the firm chooses to do not what it
must do.

12

Human Effectiveness

The effectiveness of human behavior depends on the value of its outcome. Since different parties can place different values on the same outcome, individuals may be effective in relation to their own objectives but not to the objectives of the organization of which they are part, or vice versa.

Consequently, when evaluating a person's effectiveness it is essential to ask: Effectiveness for whom? If the objectives of employees are in conflict with those of the organization of which they are part, then they behave effectively for themselves or the organization but not for both. Therefore, *the effectiveness of employees can be maximized only if their values and those of the organization are not in conflict.*

An industrial enterprise places value on employees' *productivity* and *the quality of their output*. Unless employees themselves value the amount and quality of their output, they may not behave as effectively as they might from the organization's point of view. Maximization of employees' effectiveness, however, does not require that they value productivity and product quality as ends in themselves. This is not necessary if *they value the organization and believe that it values productivity and product quality*. They will try to provide the organization with what it wants. People do things for friends that they prefer not to do, but they do them because of the satisfaction they believe their actions give their friends.

The amount of satisfaction we derive from satisfying others is directly proportional to the amount of satisfaction they provide us. This is the reason that quality-of-work-life programs are directed at making work more satisfying and fulfilling. Such work makes employees value the organization that provides it, even if they do not value its ends.

Because industrial enterprises want more productivity and quality of product from employees, measures of these variables are commonly used as measures of human effectiveness. Such measurement can be difficult, however. Productivity and quality of output are affected by many things other than human effort; for example, the technology and the quality of the raw materials used. Separation of an individual's contribution from that of a change in technology or raw material may not be easy but it is seldom impossible.

Measurement of the effectiveness of an organization from

the point of view of its employees is more difficult. It is usually done indirectly by use of such indicators as absenteeism, lateness, incidents of sabotage, attrition rates, actions requiring discipline, and accidents. In recent years surveys of the attitudes of employees have been used increasingly. These surveys are often conducted annually to detect changes in attitudes and their sources.

Quality-of-work-life programs are directed toward improving attitudes and, by such improvement, toward increasing productivity and quality of product. These programs are not cost-free. Although their advocates claim their costs are more than justified, every organization should determine for itself whether this is the case. It can be done by small-scale experiments in which troublesome work groups, white- or blue-collar, are exposed to these programs. Then measures of effectiveness of the individuals involved from the point of view of the organization and of the organization from the point of view of the individuals can be made before and after initiation of the programs. Repeating these measurements periodically and analyzing them helps an organization learn how to increase its own effectiveness and that of its employees.

REFLECTIONS

Firms and its employees may have objectives that are in conflict. Firms may value productivity & quality. Measurement of human effectiveness by measurement of quality and productivity may not be the best way to measure productivity & quality. Employees measure organization effectiveness by means of their value & quality of work life. Periodic measurements need to be made to determine organization effectiveness and effectiveness of the employees.

13

Quality of Work Life

Many corporate efforts are being made to increase the productivity of labor and the quality of its output. Some of these efforts have been successful; some have not. My experience suggests that certain characteristics make the difference, characteristics that convert into 10 commandments. Violation of any one of them may be enough to spell failure.

First, *labor-oriented programs should not focus on increasing productivity and product quality but on the satisfaction derived from work*. They should focus on the *quality of work life*, not the quantity and quality of work. If job satisfaction is increased, productivity and product quality usually increase by considerably more than the programs that focus on them can bring about.

Second, *the quality of the work life of managers at all levels should be improved before labor is dealt with.* Wherever this has been done subsequent programs for the workforce have been better supported by managers at all levels. Wherever this has *not* been done middle and lower levels of management often obstruct programs directed at labor.

Third, *once managers are taken care of the quality-of-work-life program should be extended to cover all white- and blue-collar workers.* Participation in these programs should be voluntary for everyone but managers; their participation should be a condition of their employment.

Fourth, *managers and workers should be prepared for these programs by receiving instruction in cooperative group processes, and this should be done on company time.* Effective groups seldom come about naturally.

Fifth, *once the programs are initiated, discipline should be directed at correcting undesirable behavior rather than punishing it.* Punishment seldom produces good behavior that lasts, and even less frequently produces a satisfied worker.

Sixth, *discipline of those who break the rules should be applied regardless of rank.* No double standards; the discipline applied to managers and nonmanagerial personnel should be the same.

Seventh, *commitments made by any participant in a quality-of-*

work-life program should be followed up and met. If a participant cannot meet a commitment, a complete explanation
for the failure should be given to the other parties.

Eighth, *the breaking up of labor–management meetings into cau-
cuses should be discouraged.* To the extent possible, all
discussion should take place openly in joint meetings.

Ninth, *an experienced and competent third party should be engaged,* initially at least, *to facilitate joint meetings and to provide general guidance in the process.* The third party should
be subject to approval by the other two and dismissible by
either one.

Tenth and most important, *the quality-of-work-life programs
should not be designed or redesigned by experts but by those directly affected by them.* Lower level employees are wary of
experts, especially those employed by management, and
suspect their programs of being instruments of exploita-
tion. Unfortunately, their suspicions are often justified.

REFLECTIONS

Programs should be focused on improving job satisfaction
attitude and quality of work life. Then productivity
and quality usually come along. Start with
managers at all levels and to the labor.

14

Incentives

Tied Performance Measurement

Incentives are widely used to influence behavior that cannot be controlled. Frequently, however, they do not work or work in unintended ways; for example, a large producer of home appliances also installs and services these appliances. Company employed servicemen equipped with vans call at the homes of users requiring service. The company's management became concerned about the large parts inventory carried in these vans, particularly because servicemen normally used only a few parts per day.

A research organization was employed to try to reduce this mobile inventory. Researchers learned that the servicemen were paid for each repair call they made. If they did not have the parts to complete an installation or repair, they had to go to a warehouse to get them. This could take two to four hours for which they received no compensation. No wonder they carried every part they might possibly need. The way the repairmen were paid was an unintended incentive to their carrying large numbers of parts.

Some incentive systems are seriously misconceived because their objectives are not clearly formulated; for example, two major cities decided independently to reduce traffic congestion by charging automobiles and trucks for using the streets. They developed very different proposals for imposing these charges. One planned to base them on the number of miles driven within the city, the other, on the frequency with which vehicles appropriately marked passed electronic eyes that could read identification numbers inscribed on their sides. An argument developed between the transportation planners of these cities regarding the merits of each system. They decided to employ a research organization to make a comparative evaluation of their designs.

At the planners' first meeting with the researchers one researcher asked for the purpose of the proposed systems. Surprised by an apparently naive question, a planner explained that the objective was obviously to reduce congestion. The researcher then asked, "What is congestion?" An increasingly annoyed planner replied, "Everybody knows what congestion is." The persistent researcher said "Not everybody; I don't." The thoroughly impatient planner rose, went to a window, pointed down to the street, and said, "Look, you can see it." The researcher then asked the planner what he saw. The planner blurted, "For God's sake, the cars aren't moving." "Ah," said the researcher, "then what you want to reduce is the number of cars *not* moving on the streets. Then why are you proposing to charge them for moving?"

The researcher then pointed out to the flabbergasted planner that if he wanted to reduce congestion, it would be better to charge drivers for the number of times they stopped than for how much they moved. Such a charge, he pointed out, would induce them to use their vehicles at off hours and on less congested routes. Moreover, stops could be counted less expensively (by a simple inertial meter) than moving could be measured.

Another city, connected to most of its suburbs by bridges and tunnels, wanted to reduce the number of cars driven by commuters. It proposed to increase the average charges by imposing a fee per car plus a fee for each passenger in each car. A consultant pointed out that this would induce drivers not to carry passengers, hence would increase the number of cars. To reduce the number of cars using bridges and tunnels, he said, a fee should be charged for each *empty seat*. This would induce car pooling and the use of smaller cars. (Cars carrying three or more passengers can now travel at no cost in express lanes on the San Francisco Bay Bridge.)

Because incentives so frequently produce unexpected results, it is worth having them reviewed critically by at least a sample of those they are intended to affect, and this should be done *before* they are implemented.

Incentives will not serve their intended purposes unless they also serve the purposes of those they are intended to affect.

REFLECTIONS

Incentives are widely used to increase desired behavior. But incentives often produce unexpected results; when designing incentive programs one must critically evaluate the program & know what kind of behavior or objective do they want to promote & see if a propose program will enhance those kind of behavior. The incentive must serve the purpose or have value to those who are intended to affect.

15

The Resurrection of A&P

Between 1974 and 1982 the Great Atlantic & Pacific Tea Company (A&P) closed about 2500 of its stores; 60 of them were in the Philadelphia area. Blame was placed on labor costs, which had been about 5 percent higher than the industry average.

Local 1357 of the United Food and Commercial Workers, a major victim of these closings, lost thousands of members. Wendell Young, the local's president, asked the Busch Center of The Wharton School to determine whether it would be possible for some of the workers who had lost their jobs to buy and operate stores abandoned by A&P. A study was conducted with positive results. When the local issued a call for volunteers 600 members offered to put up

$5000, the amount required of each, and two stores were purchased from A&P. Helped by the Busch Center, the worker–owners prepared a detailed design of the operation and management of the stores. From the day they opened the O&O (Owned and Operated) stores showed better performance than the A&P stores had realized in the same sites.

O&O's success prompted A&P to reevaluate its failure and to suggest a study to determine whether their stores could be redesigned to make them viable. With the help of the Busch Center a joint effort that involved company management, the local, and a number of workers was launched. A *Quality of Work Life Plan* was produced, on the basis of which A&P agreed to reopen 20 stores. By mutual agreement these stores were to be part of a new subsidiary of A&P called "Super Fresh." The following conditions were critical parts of the agreement:

1. The workers accepted shorter vacations and pay cuts up to $2 an hour.

2. The workers would receive 1 percent of gross sales if the labor costs were no more than 10 percent of operating revenues and a higher percentage if they were below 9 percent.

3. Management committed itself to a Quality-of-Work-Life program, the foundation of which was employee involvement. All employees were to be members of planning boards, which were to be established for each work unit at every level of the organization and which would have a significant

amount of control over the operation of their departments, stores, or regions.

At the stores that have since been reopened workers have
the right to make dozens of decisions that were once exclusively in management's hands. They participate in decisions regarding layout, allocation of shelf space, items to
be carried, pricing and promotions, and assignment of
personnel. Workers have changed store hours, replaced
direct-mail advertising with newspaper advertising, and
discontinued slow-moving items. One store's meat department employees suggested changing the meat display
to add more soup bones next to the stew beef. Not only
did sales improve, but customers did not "ring the bell" so
often. Prompted by employees, an intercom system was
installed at registers to allow check-out clerks to price an
unmarked item with less delay.

The Wall Street Journal of September 29, 1983, quoted
Gerald Goode, president of Super Fresh, as saying: "We
don't have employees at our stores. We have associates."

Twenty-four Super Fresh stores, employing 2105 workers,
were opened in the last five months of 1982. These stores
reported record sales and profits from the start. The chain
is growing more rapidly than any other in the Delaware
Valley.

. . . while competitors complain, Super Fresh continues to
open stores at such a rapid clip that it is beginning to run
out of prime locations. As of this week, 45 of the 79 area
markets that once were A&P stores have reopened as Su-

per Fresh markets and eight to 12 more are expected to be opened by July 1. (*Philadelphia Inquirer*, April 3, 1983.)

Little wonder that the Super Fresh format is now being used to convert existing A&P stores and to reopen others that had been closed.

The resurrection of A&P as Super Fresh suggests, first, new collaborative and entrepreneurial roles for unions in the revitalization of dying or dead businesses; second, that managers are learning how to make better use of the knowledge and good will of their workers; and, finally, that third parties can enable two parties locked in mortal combat to find creative win-win ways of dissolving their differences.

REFLECTIONS

Business tend to have a negative attitude toward unions. They view unions as a plague that stuck on their back. Union have displayed that all they can offer to business is more incentives for employees. If both side can change their attitude & behaviors they may be able to accomplish things together.

16

Paternalism

A large number of business enterprises are still seeking to become a "great big happy family." Not surprisingly, these organizations tend to be managed paternalistically by an "old man" at the top. Authority is concentrated in the "Father" who dispenses it downward. Such chief executives can revoke or revise any decisions made at any level below them. Therefore, decisions to be made tend to be pushed up the organizational ladder as far as possible. They are often made by managers who are far removed from the area directly affected and who lack the information and knowledge required to make them well.

Patronage is commonplace in paternalistic organizations. *Who* one knows is usually more important than *what* one knows. This provides those who are patronized with a convenient way of avoiding responsibility. By obtaining approval from above before acting they absolve themselves of responsibility for what they eventually do. Their guiding principle seems to be: *Don't make any decision that you can get someone higher to make for you.* As a result, even routine decisions often require inordinate amounts of time. In contrast, requests from above are acted on at once. The higher the source of a request, the less time required for a response.

In a paternalistic organization time is allocated to work through a priority system based on the rank of the person requesting it. This raises havoc with schedules and appointments. Anyone can be bumped from a schedule because someone higher wants that time. (The higher authority is never informed of the "bump.") Appointments are often canceled at the last moment or not kept. Lateness is the rule. Waiting is an organizational pastime. The higher the rank of a manager, the larger the waiting room.

The "Father" is often a workaholic who puts in long days and weeks and seldom takes a vacation. His work schedule has a rippling effect on the rest of the organization, for he expects his subordinates to be there whenever he wants them. As a result, the family life and health of subordinates frequently suffer. Their advancement often depends more on the amount of time they spend at work than on the amount of work they do.

The principal shortcoming of paternalistic organizations is

revealed in an apparently unrelated episode that occurred in a university's psychological clinic. A four-year-old son of two university professors was brought in by his parents because, they said, he hardly ever spoke. He did, however, understand all that was said to him. The parents thought their child might be retarded.

The clinician put the child through a battery of nonverbal tests and found him to have superior intelligence. These results, together with information obtained by monitoring the behavior of the parents in the child's presence, suggested a treatment. The clinician had observed that whenever he asked the child a question one of the parents immediately answered for him. The clinician advised the parents not to talk to or for the child for the next few weeks. The parents followed this advice. When they returned to the clinic the child was speaking fluently.

Paternalism breeds paralysis of the tongue, if not the mind. It ignores the fact that it is often better to do things for one's self, no matter how badly, than to have them done by others, no matter how well. People generally learn more from their own mistakes than they do from the correct decisions of others. To be sure, in some cases "father knows best," but it should be borne in mind that father is fallible.

Moreover, *paternalistic organizations are even more fallible than their fathers.*

REFLECTIONS

Paternalism can lead to inability for lower level employees to develope & they become dependent or mindless upon upper level mgmt. Mgr. who make decisions are know less about the issues & decisions they made have less effect on them than on the employees.

17

Corruption

Although corruption is widely believed to be evil, it is widely tolerated. Like the weather, more is said than done about it.

The damage to the development efforts of organizations and societies that is caused by corruption is often well hidden. It can do much more than obstruct these efforts; it can completely subvert them. Consider the case of CONASUPO, the National Basic Commodity Agency of Mexico.

One of the purposes for which CONASUPO was created was to increase the income of peasants (*campesinos*). It initiated a price-support program for such crops as corn, wheat, and beans. Each year, before these crops were planted, CONASUPO announced prices at which they would be purchased by the government if they met minimal quality standards. These prices were higher than those paid by local buyers who as a rule were affluent merchants and often the only source of provisions and supplies and the credit required to buy them. Loans were made at exorbitant rates. In addition, these merchants were the only providers of trucks with which to haul produce to markets. Little wonder, then, that they were usually the local heads (*caciques*, or chiefs) of the ruling political party, PRI. Needless to say, their incomes were seriously threatened by CONASUPO's price-support program, but not for long.

CONASUPO set up a large number of rural buying stations to which campesinos could take their produce. Consistent with the widespread practice of patronage in Mexico, the casiques were asked to nominate candidates for the job of tending these stations. Their candidates were selected more often than not.

When the program began many campesinos took their small harvests to CONASUPO's buying stations only to have them rejected by the attendants who claimed that they did not meet the minimal quality standards. The campesinos then had no alternative but to offer their produce to the casiques, who, having been dutifully informed by attendants of its rejection, pretended to be reluctant to buy. Eventually, they "gave in" to the pleas of the campesinos and bought it, but at a much lower price than they had paid before CONASUPO's program was initiated and not without lecturing the campesinos on the cost of disloy-alty.

When the peasants withdrew, poorer and penitent, the caciques took the produce they had bought to the buying stations of CONASUPO where it had previously been re-jected and sold it to the government at a much higher price than they had paid. For this the attendants were ap-propriately rewarded.

The caciques and the buying-station attendants prospered for many years until a new administrator of CONASUPO did something about it.

Even the best intentioned development programs can be subverted by corruption, and this is as true of business en-terprises as it is of societies; for example, one large corpo-ration recently made a friendly acquisition of another com-pany as part of its diversification strategy. Both companies would have benefited if the acquisition had been made at the price the acquiring company had expected to pay for the acquired company's stock. But a member of the acquiring company's board told some of his friends about the intended acquisition and substantial amounts of the stock of the company about to be acquired were bought. This drove up the price of that stock. The increased price of acquisition diluted the acquiring company's earnings significantly. As a result, the amount that could be in-vested in improvements of the acquired company was re-duced and the development of both companies was re-tarded.

The only thing more detrimental to organizational development than corruption is tolerating it.

REFLECTIONS

Corruption will not only obstruct organization developments, it will destroy them. Corruption should not be tolerated if it is known that corruption is happening.

18

Alcoholism and Stress

Alcoholism is widely known as a cause of problems in the workplace. What is not widely known is that alcoholism is strongly related to stress produced by the workplace.

Trevor Williams, George Calhoun, and I* studied 65 adults at a treatment center for alcoholics and compared them with a matched sample of 69 nonalcoholics. We looked for evidence of differences between these groups in frequency, strength, and duration of stress.

We defined stress as a condition of people who (1) have certain expectations of themselves or others or are aware of others' expectations of them, (2) believe that these expectations are reasonable, and (3) believe that these expec-

*"Stress, Alcoholism, and Personality, *Human Relations*," **35** (6), 491–510, 1982.

tations are not being met and are not likely to be met in the future; for example, stress may be caused by failure to reach our level of aspiration or the level that others have for us. It can also be caused by our failure or that of others to do a job as well as we think it should be done.

The questionnaire we used to get at the frequency, strength, and duration of stress differentiated stress arising (1) at work, (2) at home, (3) in social life, (4) from self-imposed expectations, and (5) from expectations of others.

Alcoholics identified far more unmet expectations from every source than nonalcoholics. Alcoholics responded to their failure to meet relevant expectations with more anxiety than nonalcoholics. The anxiety they experienced was stronger than that of nonalcoholics. The peak levels of anxiety provoked by unmet expectations lasted longer in alcoholics than in nonalcoholics. (Among black alcoholics 94 percent reported persistent or continuous stress, compared with only 56 percent of black nonalcoholics.)

Of the alcoholics interviewed, 66 percent reported strong or very strong anxiety at work, whereas only 21 percent of the nonalcoholics did. The workplace was revealed as a major source of stress.

We also investigated the ways in which alcoholics and nonalcoholics cope with stress. We classified coping behavior in five categories:

1. *Consumption*, including drinking, eating, smoking, and taking drugs or medication.

2. *Aggression,* starting a fight or expressing overt hostility.

3. *Escape,* getting away from the source of stress; for example, quitting one's job or leaving home.

4. *Self-distraction,* engaging in unrelated physical or social activities to take one's mind off the problem.

5. *Miscellaneous constructive activities,* including seeking advice from others, working through one's problem on one's own, solving difficulties by cooperation with others, and praying.

Even with this crude classification of coping behavior we found striking differences among the ways in which alcoholics and nonalcoholics cope with stress. More than half the alcoholics preferred one of the *destructive* strategies, consumption or aggression, whereas more than two-thirds of the nonalcoholics preferred the two *constructive* options (self-distraction and miscellaneous constructive activities). About one-fifth of each group chose the neutral strategy of escape.

More alcoholics (88 percent) than nonalcoholics (32 percent) drank to relieve stress. The contrast was even greater among whites: more white alcoholics drank (93 percent) and smoked (83 percent) to reduce stress than nonalcoholics (31 and 35 percent). More black and white nonalcoholics (39 percent), however, used eating to cope with stress than alcoholics (15 percent). More white alcoholics (41 percent) used drugs or medication to reduce stress than white nonalcoholics (0 percent).

Summarizing, we found that in every area measured alco-

holics reported more frequent, more prolonged, and sev-
erer stress than nonalcoholics. Although work was not the
only source of stress, it was important, particularly for
blacks. Finally, alcoholics tend to cope with stress more
self-destructively than nonalcoholics.

Our work did *not* show that stress *causes* alcoholism but it
did show them to be strongly associated. Therefore, we
cannot claim that a reduction in stress will reduce alcoholism but it does seem likely. Given the strong association of
stress and alcoholism and the very high cost of alcoholism
in the workplace, it is worth some time, money, and effort
to reduce the stress generated. For this reason an
increasing number of companies have instituted employee
assistance programs in which employees who suffer from
alcoholism, drug abuse, and other personal problems can
receive expert counseling and treatment. These programs
have been shown to reduce alcoholism and drug abuse
and have more than justified their cost by increasing job
satisfaction, productivity, and product quality.

REFLECTIONS

_____

_____

_____

_____

19

Too Much Communication?

Too much of a good thing, *even communication*, is a bad thing. Unconstrained communication within corporations can improve their performance *only when their parts are not in conflict*—when their objectives are compatible and mutually reinforcing. It is apparent that in war the more opponents know about one another, the more harm they can inflict. If each side knew absolutely nothing about the other, war could not be waged.

It is commonplace for parts of a corporation to be at war among themselves, or in competition. I have heard attributed to Peter Drucker the observation that there is more competition within corporations than between them and that internal competition is often waged less ethically than external competition. When parts of the same organization compete, increased communication can reduce the performance of the organization as a whole and its parts, and obstruct growth and development.

This is illustrated by a considerably simplified version of a real case, but none of its essential properties is omitted. It involved a department store in which the two most important activities are buying and selling.

The store's chief executive decided to engage in "management by objectives." In his negotiation with the purchasing manager the executive proposed the following objective: "minimization of stock." The purchasing manager pointed out that this could be accomplished by buying nothing. They eventually settled on an alternative: "minimization of stock subject to the requirement that the store be able to meet expected demand."

In a similar session between the executive and the sales manager the sales objective was formulated as "maximization of gross sales, less selling expenses."

To facilitate pursuit of his objective the sales manager had his statistical staff derive price–demand curves from data gathered for each major product category. Each plot showed three curves (Figure 1):

1. The *optimistic* curve representing the most they could expect to sell at each price.

2. The *realistic* curve representing the average amount previously sold at each price.

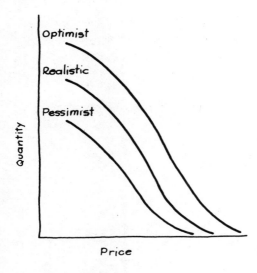

Figure 1.

3. The *pessimistic* curve representing the least they could expect to sell at each price.

Once the sales manager had selected a price (P_1) at which he intended to offer an item, he used the appropriate chart to determine how many he would need in stock (Figure 2). To do so he used the optimistic curve because he wanted to minimize sales lost because of lack of stock. Lost sales hurt his performance but excess inventory didn't. The sales manager then told the purchasing manager that he would need quantity Q_1 of the item.

The purchasing manager, who had previously served as assistant sales manager, also had access to the price–demand curves. He was told by his former subordinates in the sales department that the sales manager had used the optimistic curve; therefore, he adjusted the num-

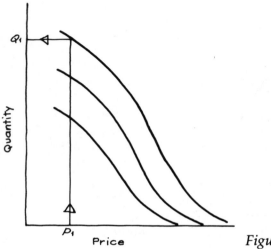

Figure 2.

ber required downward to Q_2 by using the realistic curve (Figure 3). He wanted only enough stock to meet expected demand. He let his old boss, the sales manager, know about this adjustment.

The sales manager then returned to the curves and adjusted the price upward to P_2 to maximize gross sales, given the amount of stock that would be available (Figure 4). The purchasing manager learned about this change and made a further reduction in the stock to Q_3 (Figure 5).

Had this process continued, nothing would have been bought or sold. It did not continue because the chief executive intervened by prohibiting communication about prices and stock levels between the sales and purchasing managers. This enabled the store to survive but it did not

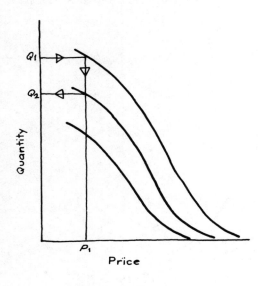

Figure 3.

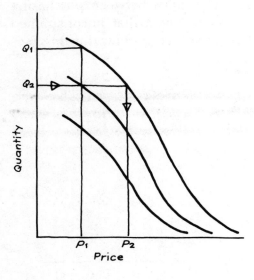

Figure 4.

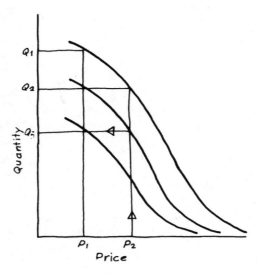

Figure 5.

thrive. It was not until the conflict between purchasing and selling objectives was removed that unconstrained communication could be permitted without hurting performance.

The moral of this fable is this: *Don't let enemies within a corporation communicate with one another, no matter how friendly they are.* Better still, *eliminate them or the conflict between them.*

REFLECTIONS

_____

_____

20

Communicating Up

Communicating up in an organization is widely recognized as more difficult and less effective than communicating down. To improve upward communication organizational gravity must be overcome. This requires removing the belief of most managers that their subordinates, unlike those of other managers, communicate with them easily and effectively. This is seldom the case.

One CEO I know learned this the hard way. He spent several weeks of each year making "state-of-the-corporation" presentations to all his company's hourly paid workers. It was a shirt-sleeve presentation, which was followed by time for questions and discussion. These sessions were always lively and gratifying to the CEO.

One year, shortly after completion of these sessions, a company-wide strike was called. The puzzled CEO asked me why none of the strike issues had been raised in any of his communication sessions. "Because," I answered, "the meetings were yours, not theirs." He asked me to explain. I told him that if he wanted to hear what the workers wanted to say, he would have to reverse roles by allowing them to organize communication sessions that he would attend. Most of what workers want to say cannot be put into short questions or comments. Even if this were possible it would be unlikely when workers must talk *up* to a boss standing in a pulpit. They must be in the pulpit and talk *down* to him. I asked the CEO if he thought he could communicate with the workers if he were part of a large audience listening to a presentation they had prepared. He got the point.

Subordinates seldom say what is on their minds even when they organize a session with their superiors. They often fear the consequences of doing so; but the openness with which they communicate to superiors can be increased in several ways.

First, a third party, one who is respected by subordinates and superiors, can help by making the presentation for the subordinates. To do this effectively the third party has to participate in the discussions in which the subordinates decide what they want to tell their superiors.

Second, sessions run by subordinates should not be used for bitching but for suggesting what superiors can do to enable them to do their work better and with more satisfaction. These sessions should be devoted to discussing what the subordinates want, not what they do not want. Getting rid of what they do not want does not necessarily get them what they want; for example, getting rid of an unwanted supervisor does not necessarily get them one they do want.

Third, meetings conducted by subordinates can lead to improvement if their superiors respond positively then and there to as many of the proposals as they can. They should commit themselves to responding to the other proposals by a designated time and stick to that commitment. Finally, when superiors cannot accept a proposal they should give a full explanation of their rejection.

Unfortunately, many managers underestimate the intelligence and goodwill of their subordinates. Those managers who get over this hurdle can communicate with their subordinates at least as well as they do with their peers.

Good *one-way* communication in organizations is not possible. Good communication must be *two-way*. The "com" in 'communicate' means *together*.

REFLECTIONS

_____

_____

_____

21

Jargon

The jargon commonly used by technicians frequently creates a chasm between them and managers.

Oscar Wilde once wrote that the United States and England are two great countries separated only by a common language. Jargon is an uncommon language that can separate even members of the same nation. Worse yet, *it can separate people from themselves;* for example, a while back I had a brilliant student, now a well-known professor at a leading university, who wrote a highly technical doctoral thesis on which he was examined by a committee of five faculty members. I chaired that session.

It was apparent from the beginning of the examination

that the candidate knew more about the subject of his thesis than any of his examiners. He answered our questions with a display of technical pyrotechnics that left us in awe.

As chairman I was the last to question him. I asked him to assume that I was an ordinary corporate manager who wanted to know what his thesis was about. Would he please explain it to me briefly?

He went to the blackboard and began to cover it with mathematical symbols. I stopped him to remind him that I was an *ordinary* manager, not a mathematician. "Oh," he said, "*that* kind of manager." He stood thoughtfully for a moment, then started over, but once again resorted to mathematical jargon. This time he stopped himself. After a long pause he said, "I'm sorry, but I can't do it. The thesis is too technical to be explained in nontechnical language."

"No," I said, "I think there's a different reason." After some thought he said, "I guess I can't do it because I don't understand what I've done well enough to explain it in nontechnical language." This time he was right.

He asked for an adjournment of the examination until he was able to deal with my question. It was granted. He returned in a week and did a great job.

Unless people can express themselves well in ordinary English, they don't know what they are talking about. It is only in ordinary English that we can communicate effectively with others and with ourselves. Communicating with ourselves is the most important kind of communication.

Jargon is noise that keeps our brains from understanding what our mouths are saying.

REFLECTIONS

_____

_____

_____

_____

·22

Computer-Controlled Managers

An increasing number of computer-based systems are being used to assist management. Managers should understand these systems well enough to know if they are doing what they are supposed to. If managers don't, they run the serious risk of being controlled by, rather than controlling, these systems; for example, a CEO of a large corporation once asked me to evaluate a document submitted to him by his computing center. It was a proposal for updating the computing equipment used primarily for a large production and inventory control system. I asked him why he hadn't evaluated the proposal himself. He said that he had tried but that he didn't understand the proposal or the system involved. I asked him why he hadn't had those who prepared the proposal explain it to him in ordinary language. He told me that this would have revealed his ignorance.

We made a bargain: I agreed to make the evaluation if he would attend a course that would enable him to make such evaluations for himself in the future.

Arrangements were made for the designers and operators of the production-inventory-control system to present their proposal to me orally.

The system they described to me at a subsequent meeting was supposed to control the production and purchasing of a large number of parts made or used at multiple locations. Nevertheless, its underlying logic was quite simple. On the basis of the previous use of each part and the time required to acquire it once it had been ordered, the system monitored its stock level and determined the level at which it should be reordered and the quantity required.

I asked the operators of the system if many items had been overstocked when the system was installed. The answer was "yes." I asked for a list of 25 of these items. Once it had been supplied, I prepared a plot for each in which the reorder level, the reorder quantity, and therefore the maximum permissible stock level were identified. Then I plotted the end-of-the-week inventories of each of the 25 parts since the initiation of the control system. I found that almost half of the items whose stock was over the maximum level when the program was begun had been reordered repeatedly when they reached their maximum stock level. This meant that the average inventory levels of these items were considerably higher than they had been before the system was installed. The system's operators had been completely unaware of it.

I went on to discover that the system was doing a number of other things it was not intended to do. It was out of control and in ways that most managers would easily have discovered had it been hand-operated.

No manager should use a system, computerized or not, whose operations are not thoroughly understood. The manager need not know how the computer works but must know what it does. Those who designed the system should be required to explain it to the manager in a language that can be understood, so its performance can be evaluated.

Every manager who uses computer-based systems should become computer literate. This is not difficult to do, nor does it take a lot of time. A manager who is familiar with the computer and the systems that are on it may well see possibilities for new systems and improvements in the old ones that the experts may have missed.

No manager has the right to allow a system to take control rather than serve. Ignorance does not excuse failure to fulfill a responsibility.

REFLECTIONS

_____

_____

_____

· 23

Management Misinformation Systems

A large number of the management information systems in operation have failed to meet the expectations of the managers they are supposed to serve. For this reason reference to them as *MISs* seems particularly appropriate.

There are many reasons for the disappointing performance of MISs. For one, their design and operation are usually based on the assumption that the most critical need of managers is for *more relevant information*. This is *not* true. They have a greater need for *less irrelevant information*, and this is not a mere play on words.

Studies of the amount of reading material managers receive have shown that they could not possibly take in all of it even if they did nothing else at work. They suffer from *information overload*. Other studies have shown that the greater the overload, the less reading done. Therefore, the more information provided to overloaded managers, the less they use.

What most managers need is a *filter* to eliminate irrelevant data. Few MISs do any filtering. Moreover, the relevant information that most managers receive requires more time to read than it should. It ought to be *condensed*.

The need for filtration and condensation is illustrated by an experiment that my colleagues and I conducted many years ago. We prepared a list of articles from recent issues of the principal journals in one branch of applied science. The list was sent to a large number of practitioners with the request that they indicate which articles they had read and which of them were above and below average. From their responses we selected four papers that were unanimously evaluated as above average and four similarly evaluated as below.

These eight articles were given to two professional science editors who were asked to reduce them by one-third only by eliminating words, sentences, or paragraphs and to do so with minimal loss of content. When they had completed this task they were asked to reduce their already reduced versions by half. Finally, they were asked to prepare short abstracts of each article. This provided us with four versions: 100, 67, 33, and 5 percent.

While these condensations were being prepared we wrote

to the authors of the articles to tell them that our students were being required to read their articles. Because, we said, we wanted to be sure our students understood the articles as intended, we asked them to prepare an objectively gradable test of the students' comprehension. All the authors complied.

Using a carefully designed experiment, we had each of a group of students read a 100 percent version of one article, a 67 percent version of another, and 33 percent and 5 percent abstract versions of others. No two students read the same four versions of the same four articles but each version of each article was read by the same number of students. Each student was then given four author-prepared examinations on the articles read.

For the above-average articles there were no significant differences in the scores obtained by those who had read the 100, 67, and 33 percent versions. Those who had read only the abstracts obtained a lower average score. This showed that even good scientific writing could be reduced by at least two-thirds without much loss of content.

In addition, there were no significant differences in the scores obtained by those who had read the 100, 67, and 33 percent versions of the below-average articles; but those who had read only the abstract obtained a *higher* average score. This showed that *the optimal length of a bad message is zero*.

Computerized systems that filter and condense information are available but seldom incorporated into MISs.

Studies of the information managers receive show that about two-thirds of it is unsolicited. Nevertheless, virtually no MISs handle these externally imposed inputs.

Good secretaries serve as filters and condensers of solicited and unsolicited information. Little wonder, then, that few managers are willing to swap their secretaries for *misses*.

REFLECTIONS

_____

_____

_____

_____

24

Mathemanagement

The use of mathematical models to solve management problems emerged out of World War II and became the preoccupation of the field called operations research (OR) or management science (MS). These models have been on the decline in the last decade. It is important for managers to know why.

About a decade ago an operations research group, highly placed in an important government agency in a third-world country, asked me to review one of its major projects. Most of the members of this group had received advanced degrees in OR from major universities in the United States.

The project involved the distribution of grains from government-operated collection points to processing centers and from these centers to food producers and wholesale and retail establishments throughout the country. The researchers were very proud of the number of variables and constraints included in the linear programming model they had developed, but they complained about their inability to obtain the quality or quantity of data their model required. To make up for this deficiency they had engaged in what is called "data enrichment," a euphemism for "data fabrication."

In evaluating their model the researchers had compared the costs of the solutions it yielded with the costs of the solutions obtained by managers without it. They had used their model to calculate the costs of the solutions being compared. Because their solutions minimized the sum of the costs *included in their model,* they had to come out better than those of the managers.

The minimization of the sum of costs included in a model is not the same as minimizing the sum of costs in the real world *unless the model is a perfect representation of reality.* It never is. All models are simplifications of reality. If this were not the case, they would be much more difficult—perhaps too difficult—to use. Therefore, it is critical to determine how well models represent reality before using them. In this project the researchers had failed to make this determination.

I also learned that the managers to whom the research

team's solutions were submitted invariably modified them to take into account variables that were not included in the model. However, the team had neither identified these variables nor made any effort to incorporate them in their model. When I asked why they told me that the variables added by managers were qualitative and therefore could not be used.

Finally, I learned that after a few months the managers had stopped using the solutions provided by the model because their political environment had changed. The changes, the researchers told me, could not be included in their model because they were neither measurable nor predictable.

Clearly, if the researchers had solved a problem, it was not the one the managers had.

Unfortunately, most managers are not equipped to evaluate the mathematical models that technicians apply to their problems or the solutions these models yield. Too many managers accept these models and solutions because of their blind faith in "quantitative methods." Managers should never use "solutions" that are extracted from models they do not understand. Nor should they stand in awe of mathematics. Rather they should be aware of how awful its products can be.

REFLECTIONS

_____

_____

_____

_____

25

Management Consultants

No profession seems to have so many professional consultants available to it as management. These consultants, like all others, fall into three main categories, defined by the same criteria used to divide labor in an organization. These criteria are *input*, *output*, and *markets*.

Labor organized by input is functionally divided; for example, into purchasing, maintenance, manufacturing, and marketing. Labor organized by output is divided by products or services; for example, the Chevrolet, Pontiac, Oldsmobile, Buick, and Cadillac divisions of General Motors. Finally, labor organized by markets is divided by geography—North, Central, and South America—or by type of customer—national accounts, wholesalers, retailers, and direct sales.

Management consultants are oriented correspondingly. Input-oriented consultants are identified by the tools, techniques, and methods they use to solve problems; for example, applied mathematicians, statisticians, computer programmers, accountants, and operations researchers.

Output-oriented consultants are identified by their product, the problems they solve; for example, designers of compensation or incentive systems, management information systems, or automated office systems. These professionals usually have available a greater variety of tools, techniques, and methods than input-oriented professionals but they tend to be less sophisticated technically.

Finally, consultants who are market-oriented are identified by the class of users they try to serve. They deal with any type of problem their users may have, employing whatever tools, techniques, and methods appear to be appropriate; for example, general practitioners of medicine. In contrast, medical specialists are output-oriented and medical technicians (e.g., radiologists) are input-oriented. General-purpose management consultants, like general practitioners of medicine, are market-oriented.

Output-oriented consultants frequently consult input-oriented consultants and market-oriented consultants frequently consult both. Yet such consultation seldom goes the other way.

Professions can evolve in either direction, changing from one type to another. Operations research (OR) is a case in point.

During World War I, when OR came into existence, and perhaps for a decade thereafter, it was a market-oriented profession. Pure and applied scientists and engineers worked on whatever problems were given to them by military commanders and, later, by corporate executives and public administrators. Not only did they apply scientific techniques and methods, but they also made liberal use of raw intelligence and common sense.

Immediately after the war corporations in the United States and Europe were confronted with accumulated demands for products that had become scarce. To meet these demands production facilities had to be converted from military to civilian production, expanded, and used efficiently. This brought up questions for which OR developed effective answers.

By the early 1960s Western industry had overexpanded its production capacity. As a result competition for satisfying the demands that existed and creation of new demand preoccupied corporate management. OR was not well equipped to deal with these marketing problems: its instruments were better suited to the study of the machinelike behavior of factories than the purposeful behavior of consumers. Most OR practitioners stayed with the problems they could handle well and further developed the instruments for dealing with them. OR gradually converted from a market-oriented to an output-oriented profession that, together with its familiar routines, was pushed down to the lower levels of management.

This degradation continued. By the early 1970s the nature of the problems confronting corporate management had once again changed. When corporations reached the limits to growth by manipulating marketing variables, further growth could be obtained only by acquisitions, mergers, joint ventures, internal development of new products and services, or foreign expansion. OR was even less applicable to these problems than it was to those in marketing. These growth- and development-related situations required strategic planning rather than operational and tactical problem solving. As a result OR continued to move down in corporations and, in many cases, out.

During its descent from the corporate executive level to lower and lower levels of management, OR focused almost exclusively on the development of its tools, techniques, and methods. It became an input-oriented profession. Its journals reflect this; they are almost completely devoid of case studies or discussion of the problems confronting corporate management. OR's dissociation from the world of management is now almost complete.

Input-oriented consultants become obsolete when their tools do. Output-oriented consultants become obsolete when the work in which they specialize becomes less important or disappears entirely. Therefore, if management consulting is to be a vibrant and developing profession, it must focus on its users and change with their needs.

Those who serve management should focus on those they serve, not on the services they render or the instruments used in rendering them.

REFLECTIONS

_____

_____

_____

_____

26

Types of Problems

There is no such thing as a marketing, production, financial, personnel, or distribution problem. Such modifiers in front of the word "problem" tell us *absolutely nothing* about its nature, but they do tell us something.

A while ago some professors at my university met with leaders of a self-development effort being made by a nearby neighborhood. A member of the community broke into the meeting with bad news. That morning an 83-year-old woman who lived in the neighborhood and was active in the development effort had gone to the area's only free health clinic for her monthly checkup. She had been told she was fine and left for home, a fourth-floor walkup.

While climbing the third flight of stairs she had a heart attack and died.

The silence that followed this announcement was finally broken by the professor of community medicine who said, "I told you we need more doctors at the clinic. If we had them, we'd be able to make house calls and this sort of thing wouldn't happen." After another silence the professor of economics spoke up: "You know, there are plenty of doctors in Philadelphia who still make house calls. She just couldn't afford one. If welfare or medical benefits were adequate, she could have called one and this wouldn't have happened." The professor of architecture then asked why elevators weren't required in all multiple-dwelling units of more than three floors.

What kind of problem was this—medical, economic, or architectural? Actually, none of these. It was just a problem. The adjectives are indicative only of the *point of view*, the *mind-set*, of the person looking at the problem.

When trouble is found in one part of an organization, say marketing, it is usually called a marketing problem. Then the effort to solve it is confined to manipulating marketing variables. This, however, is often *not* the most effective way of handling it.

Consider an industrial example. The manager of a paper mill found that its output was decreasing seriously because of an increase in the number of different types of paper the plant had to produce. This reduced the length of production runs and increased the amount of time required for setups. Therefore, the production manager saw this as a production-scheduling problem.

Because the problem was caused by an increase in the number of products in the product line, the research team he called on for help asked why that number had not been reduced, particularly when many of the products were not profitable. The production manager replied that the content of the product line was not his responsibility; it was marketing's. Despite his opposition to its doing so, the team made its proposal to the marketing manager. He rejected it because, he said, most unprofitable products were bought by consumers of profitable products. He didn't want to risk losing those customers.

The research team then took another tack; it developed a profit-based compensation system for salesmen to replace the existing system which was based on dollar volume. The new system provided no commission for unprofitable sales but increased commissions for those that were profitable. The company implemented this system. As a result the salesmen sold fewer of the unprofitable products and more of those that were profitable. Their incomes and company profits increased and production improved by more than four times as much as it could have with perfect sales forecasting and production scheduling.

What kind of problem was this—production scheduling, product-line design, or salesmen compensation? None of these; it was just a problem.

Wherever problems appear they should be looked at from

as many different points of view as possible before a way of attacking them is selected. *The best place to solve a problem is not necessarily where it appears.*

REFLECTIONS

_____

_____

_____

_____

27

Problem Treatments

There are four ways of treating problems: *absolution, resolution, solution,* and *dissolution.*

To *absolve* a problem is to ignore it and hope it will go away or solve itself.

To *resolve* a problem is to do something that yields an outcome that is good enough, that *satisfies*. Problem resolvers take a *clinical* approach to problems; they rely heavily on experience, trial and error, qualitative judgments, and common sense. They try to identify the cause of a problem, remove or suppress it, and thereby return to a previous state.

To *solve* a problem is to do something that yields the best possible outcome, that *optimizes*. Problem solvers take a *research* approach to problems. They rely heavily on experimentation and quantitative analysis.

To *dissolve* a problem is to eliminate it by *redesigning* the system that has it. Problem dissolvers try to *idealize*, to approximate an ideal system and thereby do better in the future than the best that can be done now.

The differences between these approaches is illustrated by the following case. A large city in Europe uses double-decker buses for public transportation. Each bus has a driver and a conductor. The driver is seated in a compartment separated from the passengers. The closer the driver keeps to schedule, the more he is paid. The conductor collects zoned fares from boarding passengers, issues receipts, collects these receipts from disembarking passengers, and checks them to see that the correct fare has been paid. He also signals the driver when the bus is ready to move on after stopping to receive or discharge passengers. Undercover inspectors ride the buses periodically to determine whether conductors collect all the fares and check all the receipts. The fewer misses they observe the more the conductors are paid.

To avoid delays during rush hours, conductors usually let passengers board without collecting their fares and try to collect them between stops. Because of crowded conditions on the bus they cannot always return to the entrance in time to signal the driver to move on. This causes delays that are costly to the driver. As a result hostility has grown between drivers and conductors which has resulted in a number of violent episodes.

Management of the system first tried to ignore the problem, hoping that if it were left alone it would absolve itself. This effort at absolution did not work; the situation got worse.

Management then tried to resolve the problem by proposing a return to an earlier state by eliminating incentive payments and accepting less on-schedule performance. The drivers and the conductors rejected this proposal because it would have reduced their earnings.

Next management tried to solve the problem by having the drivers and conductors on each bus share equally the sum of the incentive payments due each. This proposal was also rejected by drivers and conductors; they were opposed to cooperating in any way.

Finally, a problem dissolver was employed by management to deal with the situation. Instead of trying to compromise the conflicting interests of the drivers and conductors, he decided to take a broader view of the system. He found that during rush hours there were more buses in operation than there were stops in the system. Therefore, at his suggestion, conductors were moved off the buses at peak hours and placed at the stops. This reduced the number of conductors required at peak hours and made it possible to improve the distribution of their working hours. Under the new system conductors collected fares during peak hours from people waiting for buses and were always at the rear entrance to signal drivers to move on. At off-peak hours, when the number of buses in operation was fewer than the number of stops, conductors returned to the buses.

The problem was dissolved.

To problem dissolvers problems are opportunities, not threats. By redesigning the systems with the problems, a better performance than the best currently possible can be obtained.

REFLECTIONS

_____

_____

_____

_____

28

Creativity

Everyone would like to be creative, but what is creativity? I believe it is *the ability to identify self-imposed constraints, remove them, and explore the consequences of their removal.* This is the same ability required to solve puzzles. Puzzles are problems that are difficult to solve precisely because of self-imposed constraints; for example, consider the nine-dot puzzle that many of us tried to solve as children. The nine dots form a square. The instructions are to place a pen or pencil on any one of the dots and, without raising the pen or pencil from the paper, to cover all the dots with four straight lines.

If we try the most obvious "solution" to determine what

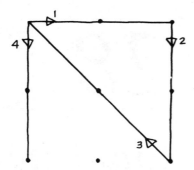

Figure 1.

the problem is (Figure 6), we leave one dot uncovered. If we try two diagonals (Figure 7), we leave two dots uncovered. This is hardly progress. The most common solution—there are many—consists of drawing lines that go *outside the perimeter of the square* (Figure 8). Many solutions can be obtained by *folding the paper*. Neither going outside the square nor folding the paper is precluded by the instructions but each is often assumed to be disallowed. Such assumptions are self-imposed constraints.

Unfortunately, knowing what creativity is does not help much in any effort to capture it. The principal difficulty lies in identifying self-imposed constraints; we are gener-

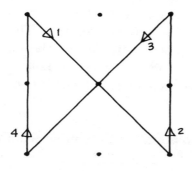

Figure 2.

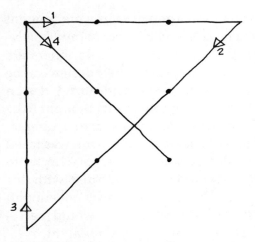

Figure 3.

ally unaware of them. There are many ways of raising them to consciousness or avoiding them even without raising them to consciousness. Among them are lateral thinking, brain-storming, synectics, TKJ, conceptual block-busting, and idealized redesign, the last of which, I believe, is the most effective.

An idealized redesign is one prepared on the assumption that the system was destroyed last night but that its environment remains intact. It is this assumption that removes most self-imposed constraints.

The product of idealized redesign is a design of that system with which the designers would *now* replace the system assumed to have been destroyed; that is, if they were *completely free* to do so. The only constraints placed on the design are (1) that it be *technologically feasible*, to preclude science fiction, and (2) that it be *operationally viable*, capable of surviving in the current environment *if* it were brought into existence. However, *the design need not be capable of being brought into existence.* Nevertheless, the designers are almost always surprised at how closely their design can be approximated. The reason is that the idealized design process clearly reveals that many constraints thought to be externally imposed are actually self-imposed; for example, in 1973 the Fourth District Federal Reserve Bank was faced with an exponentially increasing number of checks to clear. It did not see how it could continue to deal with this increase for more than a few years. There was not enough space to house all the check clearers that would be required. No way out of the difficulty was apparent.

The Bank's management decided to prepare an idealized redesign of the money-exchange system. It began by observing that a check is nothing but a way of transmitting information between banks. Was this the best way? Once this question was asked, the designers were able to remove a self-imposed constraint: the assumption that the transfer of funds between bank accounts requires the use of checks. On reflection it became apparent that this transfer could be done electronically. As a result an electronic funds transfer system, a version of which is now widely used, was designed. This system has significantly reduced the rate of growth of the number of checks that require processing, thereby eliminating what was once an impending crisis.

To idealize is to think without constraints. *To think without constraints is to think creatively.*

REFLECTIONS

_____

_____

_____

_____

29

Beating the System

If I could add only one subject to business-school curricula it would be on *how to beat the system*. Beating the system means making a well-designed system work poorly or a poorly designed system work well.

Recall that British workers found an effective way to keep the organizations that employed them from functioning well: *working to rule*. What is not so well known is that if managers went strictly "according to the book," they too would keep their organizations from functioning well. Breaking some of the rules some of the time and getting away with it—beating the system—is essential to the effectiveness, if not the survival, of even the best organizations.

Does this mean that something is inherently wrong with all the rules imposed by organizations on their employees? No, not all, but many. Those who make the rules often assume that those subjected to them are not capable of exercising good judgment. Therefore, most rules are made without allowing for exceptions and there are justifiable exceptions to every rule; for example, the Federal Aviation Authority has imposed the rule that seat backs in an airplane must be in a forward position on takeoff and landing. This maximizes the distance between the backs of seats and the faces of the persons sitting behind them, and it permits passengers to get out of their seats and into the aisle more easily in an emergency. But if there were no one seated in the row behind a passenger, the rule would make no sense. If a plane is going to hit something, it is best to be as close as possible to a reclining position, with feet forward and resting against something solid. Nevertheless, when flight attendants work to rule they create a potential risk to some passengers.

To cite a corporate example, an R&D organization works mostly on government contracts but one of its departments deals almost exclusively with corporate clients, whom the organization charges on a cost-plus basis. Until recently it applied overhead only to direct salaries of professional personnel; other expenses were charged without overhead. The organization's executive then changed its practice by applying overhead to *all* costs. This created a serious problem for the corporately oriented department which had more travel-related expenses than any other department because most of its work is done at corporate sites. If it had to apply overhead to these costs, it would lose most of its clients. To get around the new practice the head of the department had each client open accounts with the organization's travel agent and the hotels at which his department's personnel stayed when visiting their clients. The clients are now billed directly for most travel expenses, thereby avoiding the overhead. If the manager of this department had not beaten his company's charging system, he would not have the clients he has and he would not be able to serve them or his parent organization nearly as well as he does.

My course on beating the system would teach people how to break obstructive rules. One of the experts I would bring in as a guest lecturer is the neighbor of a friend. She recently told me that for years a nearby department store had cashed her checks. This had been a great convenience because the store was much closer to her home than her bank. But, she told me, this service had recently been discontinued. Nevertheless, she had figured out a way to beat its system. If she needed cash, she bought something in the store for approximately the amount she needed and paid for it by check, which was acceptable to the store. Then she immediately took her purchase to the return desk, where, in accordance with store policy, she was given a *cash* refund.

Would that all managers had her ability. Fortunately, many of them have at least some. If all managers took their budgets as literally as flight attendants take FAA regulations, most corporations would grind to a halt. Managers worth their salt know how to beat the budget and get

what they need. When this is done, organizations worth
their salt look the other way.

REFLECTIONS

_____

_____

_____

_____

30

Defending Against New Ideas

Not all new ideas presented to management are good. Defenses against the bad are necessary, but they tend to be applied to the good as well. This makes it difficult to innovate in many organizations.

Having spent many years in attacking these defenses, I am a self-proclaimed expert on the subject. Let me identify some of the most commonly used defenses.

1. *HAS THIS IDEA EVER BEEN APPLIED SUCCESSFULLY?*

is this idea any good

If the answer is "No, it is too new to have been applied," the defender will dismiss it because it has not been tested. He will not try anything that has not been done successfully by others. He is repelled by the prospect of being the first.

If the answer is "Yes," the defender will go on to the second defense.

2. *THE IDEA IS A GOOD ONE BUT IT DOESN'T APPLY TO OUR KIND OF BUSINESS OR IN OUR KIND OF ENVIRONMENT*

is this idea any good to our organization

The naïve presenter usually responds to this defense by citing a case of a business or an environment similar to the defender's in which the idea has been applied successfully. The defender then points out the inevitable differences between any two businesses or environments.

This sequence could be continued indefinitely, but eventually the presenter or the defender will give up without changing his mind. To paraphrase Ambrose Bierce: there is always an infinite number of reasons for not doing something, but only one for doing it: it is *right*. But this is hard to prove to someone who prefers to do nothing.

Even when the "offender" overwhelms the defender with successful cases the battle is not won. The third line of defense is called into play.

3. HAVE ANY APPLICATIONS OF YOUR IDEA FAILED? *attacking your credential on*

If the answer is "Yes," the response is "Aha! I thought so," and the idea is dismissed. If the answer is "No," the defender clearly doesn't believe it and dismisses the idea.

Defenses 1, 2, and 3 are used by those who accept the novelty of the idea presented. If its novelty is not accepted, different defenses are used.

4. THIS IS NOTHING BUT . . .

In the early 1950s, when operations research was new, I collected 14 assertions that it was "nothing but . . . ." It was said to be identical to such diverse disciplines as industrial engineering, economics, statistics, applied mathematics, and cybernetics. Therefore, I formulated the following definition: "Operations research is a field that is identical to each of 14 fields, each of which is different from all the others." This definition had no effect on the "this-is-nothing-but-ers." Nothing does.

The "old-stuffers" are equally intransigent.

5. WE TRIED IT A LONG TIME AGO AND IT DIDN'T WORK THEN. WHY SHOULD IT NOW?

I once presented a newly developed mathematical technique that could be used to solve a serious problem that had long faced the managers I addressed. One of them told me he had tried the technique 20 years earlier and it hadn't worked then. I naïvely pointed out how recently it had been invented and that he could not have used the same technique that long ago. He told me that the inventor had obviously rediscovered the wheel. I gave up.

If an "old-stuffer" can't refer to his own imagined experience with an idea, he refers to that of others.

6. (SUCH AND SUCH A) COMPANY TRIED THIS IDEA AND IT DIDN'T WORK THERE. WHY SHOULD IT HERE?

More than a decade ago Volvo built its radically new assembly plant in Kalmar, Sweden. Representatives of the American automotive industry and business journalists went to examine it. Almost without exception they reported that it was not working or would not work in the United States. A decade later, when the American automotive industry was in dire straights, it reevaluated Kalmar and has since imitated it increasingly.

Alas! There is nothing new under the sun or in the way managers defend themselves against new ideas.

REFLECTIONS

_____

_____

_____

_____

31

The Obvious

When the word "obvious" is applied to an assertion it does *not* mean that the truth of the statement is so apparent that it requires no supporting evidence or argument. I learned this as a college freshman from an eminent professor of mathematics who, because of his eminence, had exclusive use of a classroom connected to his office.

One day he was going through a proof in geometry, writing the steps in one column and the supporting reasons in another. After writing the third step on the board he drew a squiggly line in the "reasons" column and told us that this step was obvious. Halfway through the next step he stopped, stepped back, and looked at the blackboard quizzically. He then turned to the class and said, "Excuse me. I'll be right back." He disappeared into his office and was gone for what seemed to be a very long time. When he returned he had a self-satisfied grin on his face. "I was right," he said, "that step was obvious."

Obviousness is a property *not* of statements that require no proof but of statements made by those who are unwilling to have them questioned.

Statements said to be obvious are often untrue. Therefore, their acceptance without questioning often obstructs effective problem solving. The following case is an illustration:

Back in the days when stewardesses had to be unmarried I was part of a team that worked for a major airline on improving the scheduling of its school in which these young women were trained. While engaged in this effort we found that on the average stewardesses flew fewer hours per month than the maximum allowed. We looked into this and eventually developed a way of scheduling stewardesses that would increase their average flying time considerably.

We presented our findings to the airline's senior managers, all of whom but the vice-president of personnel showed great enthusiasm for our proposal. This vice-president argued that an increase in flying time would increase the stewardesses' attrition rate and would cost the airline more in recruiting and training than it would save in operating costs. This had not occurred to us but we reacted in typical academic fashion. We asked, "How do you know?" He replied that it was *obvious* to anyone who had worked with stewardesses, and *obviously* we hadn't. When we pressed for more convincing proof he refused to discuss it further. Fortunately, the remaining managers were willing to discuss it further. That discussion eventually led to their authorizing our looking into the matter.

Because monthly flight assignments were selected by stewardesses in the order of their seniority, we compared the average hours of the most senior with those of the most junior. Contrary to what the vice-president of personnel had told us, we found that on the average, senior stewardesses flew *more* hours than their juniors. Further investigation revealed the reason: the senior stewardesses preferred schedules with regular days off and most free evenings at their home bases. We learned that schedules with these characteristics made it easier for them to organize their social lives and were more likely to be found in assignments with greater flying time.

We then modified our initially proposed scheduling procedure to provide all stewardesses with regularity of days off during a month and at least 20 percent more evenings at home. Despite these modifications, we were able to retain most of the increased flying time made possible by our earlier scheduling procedure. These results were presented to the stewardesses' union which supported our proposal enthusiastically and joined in submitting it to management. It was accepted and implemented. The expected reduction in the airline's costs was obtained.

This improvement in performance was almost lost because

one executive, presumed to be an authority, had said that more flying time would not be acceptable to the stewardesses and that this was *obvious*.

The great American wit Ambrose Bierce perceived all this when he defined "self-evident"—a synonym of "obvious"—as "evident to oneself and no one else."

REFLECTIONS

_____

_____

_____

_____

32

Objectivity

Objectivity is a scientific ideal particularly sought by management scientists. Although its meaning is not clear, objectivity is generally believed to be what Winnie the Pooh called a "GOOD THING." It is also believed to require the exclusion of ethical and moral judgments from inquiry and decision making. *Objectivity so conceived is not possible.*

Most, if not all, scientific inquiry involves testing hypotheses or estimating the values of variables. These procedures necessarily entail balancing two types of error. In testing hypotheses these errors are rejecting hypotheses when they are true and accepting them when they are false. Naturally we would like to minimize the probabilities of making them but unfortunately minimizing one maximizes the other. Therefore, setting these probabilities requires a judgment of the relative seriousness, hence value, of the two types of error. Researchers seldom make this judgment consciously; they usually set the probabilities at levels dictated by scientific convention. This attests not to their objectivity but to their ignorance.

The choice of a way of estimating the value of a variable requires the evaluation of the relative importance, hence values, of underestimates and overestimates of the variable. Each estimating procedure contains a (usually implicit) judgment of the seriousness of the two possible types of error. Therefore, estimates cannot be made without a value judgment, however concealed it may be.

The most commonly used estimating procedures are said to be "unbiased." The estimates they yield, however, are best only when errors of equal magnitude but of opposite sign are equally serious. This is a condition that I have virtually never found in the real world.

In testing hypotheses and estimating the values of variables, science unconsciously equates objectivity with unconsciousness of the value judgments.

The prevailing concept of objectivity is based on a distinction between ethical-moral man—who is believed to be emotional, involved, and biased—and scientific man—who is believed to be unemotional, uninvolved, and unbiased. Objective decision makers are expected to take their heads—not their hearts—into the workplace. To assume that the heart and head can be separated is like assuming that the head and tail of a coin can be separated because they can be discussed or looked at separately.

Objectivity does *not* consist of making only value-free judgments in conducting inquiries and making decisions. It consists of making only value-*full* judgments; the more extensive the values, the more objective the results. A determination is objective only if it holds for *any* values that those who can use it may have. For this reason objectivity is an ideal that can never be attained but can be continuously approached.

Objectivity cannot be approximated by an individual investigator or decision maker; it can be approached only by groups of individuals with diverse values. It is a property that cannot be approximated by individual scientists but can be by science taken as a system.

All this has an important implication for management. The values of all those affected by a decision, its *stakeholders*, should be taken into account in making that decision but this cannot be done without involving them in the decision-making process. To deprive them of opportunities to participate in making decisions that affect them is to devalue them, and this, it seems to me, is immoral. Managers have a moral obligation to *all* who can be affected by their decisions, not merely to those who pay for their services.

REFLECTIONS

_____

_____

_____

_____

33

Infallibility

Technology is all but worshiped in a large part of the world. As a result, scientists and engineers, like the clergy, are often believed to be infallible. When confronted by those who believe or tend to believe this, I usually tell them three stories.

The first is about research conducted many years ago by Dr. Tibor Fabian at the University of California, Los Angeles. Fabian had developed one of the first computerized management games. It required those who played it to manage a production process and to try to minimize the sum of production and inventory costs. A model in the computer generated the situations that required decisions as well as their consequences. It was a simple model, one with which most students of management are familiar. However, the players were not aware of this.

At a national conference of economists held in Los Angeles, Fabian offered those attending an opportunity to play the game, then a great novelty. In return, he asked the players to collect data and make an effort to derive the model that generated the decision situations and the results of their decisions. *Not one player obtained the correct model.*

The second experiment was conducted by Alex Bavelas at MIT, also many years ago. His subjects were taken into a room furnished with a screen on which slides were projected. The slides had been produced by waving a flashlight in a dark room over unexposed film. The subjects sat at desks on which there were two buttons. They were told to press one of the buttons after each slide. If they pressed the right one, they would be paid; if they pressed the wrong one, they would get nothing.

The subjects naturally asked what principle was involved in determining the right button. Bavelas told them this was what they had to find out by trial and error.

After a few slides most subjects began to formulate theories to explain the rewards they had received, and soon they were quite sure of the correct explanation. They played accordingly. If they were not rewarded as expected, they blamed it on their observations, not on their theories.

When the experiment was completed the subjects were asked to reveal their theories. All of them did so willingly. Bavelas then told them that he had actually rewarded them purely at random. There had been no relationship between the buttons they pressed and the rewards. Most of the subjects were surprised but insisted that their theories were at least approximately correct. *They would not abandon their theories.*

The third piece of research was conducted by Professors C. West Churchman and Philburn Ratoosh at the University of California, Berkeley. They too developed a management game, but theirs required play by a team of four. One acted as the CEO, the others as managers of manufacturing, marketing, and finance. The teams were asked to maximize the performance of the simulated firm. As in the Fabian experiment, this simulation was generated by a well-known mathematical model from which an optimal solution could easily be derived. Furthermore, all the graduate students who were used as subjects had attended a class on quantitative methods in which this model and its solution had been presented.

In each team the student who served as the financial manager was informed beforehand of the nature of the model and its solution. These managers, however, were told not to reveal this information to their teammates until they received a signal from the experimenter. They were then to pretend to have made the discovery on their own.

Only a small percentage of the teams adopted the optimal solution when it was proposed to them.

Churchman and Ratoosh described this experiment and its results at a large number of professional meetings, at each of which explanations of the failure of the teams to implement the optimal solution were proposed and corrective actions suggested. Churchman and Ratoosh recorded these suggestions and subsequently tested them in the same experimental situation they had already used but with new subjects. *The probability of implementation was not significantly increased.*

The morals suggested by these stories are the following, in turn:

1. *When there is regularity in nature, scientists may not find it.*

2. *When there is no regularity in nature, they may insist that there is and that they know what it is.*

3. *When there is regularity in nature and it is revealed to scientists, they may be disinclined to use it.*

Those who do not know but think they do are more dangerous advisers than those who do not know—but know it.

REFLECTIONS

_____

_____

_____

_____

34

Who's Irrational?

We often say of people whose behavior we do not expect
and cannot explain that they are *irrational*. In this way we
absolve ourselves of any responsibility for their behavior.

I have never seen a problem believed to be caused by the
behavior of others that could be solved by assuming that
they were irrational. On the other hand, by assuming that
we are irrational, solutions to these problems can often be
found; for example, during a working visit to India in 1957
I met a number of family planners from the United States
who had made no progress in their extended efforts to reduce India's birthrate. Most of them attributed their failure
to the irrationality of the Indians.

After hearing this a number of times I suggested to one of the family planners that it could be they who were irrational. I pointed out that a Brazilian woman had recently given birth to her forty-second child. Assume, I said, that the average woman can produce only about half this number, say 20. The difference between 20 and 4.6, the average number of children per Indian family, is much greater than the difference between 4.6 and 0. This, I suggested, was an indication that the size of Indian families was not due to lack of birth control.

The family planner I had addressed thought this argument was ridiculous. He left, terminating our conversation. Fortunately, a distinguished Indian demographer, T. K. Balakrishnan, approached me with apologies for having overheard our conversation. He suggested that we collaborate in research on the possible rationality of Indian reproductive behavior.

We began at the Indian Statistical Institute, but I had to return to the States before our research was finished. Luckily, Glen Camp, one of my colleagues, replaced me in India and helped Balakrishnan finish the work. Briefly, this is what they found.

The average Indian male could expect a number of years of unemployment when he got older. India had no social security program and the typical worker did not earn enough to save for these unemployed years. His only hope, then, was to be provided for by his children. It took an average of 1.1 wage earners to support one unem-

ployed adult at the minimal subsistence level, but, because it takes two to produce a child, each family needed
at least 2.2 wage-earning children. Because half the children born were female, and females were essentially un-
employable in India at that time, 4.4 children were required. To cover infant and child mortality, this number
had to be adjusted upward to 4.6 children.

This result could have been obtained by pure chance, but
its validity was easy to determine. If family size could be
explained even in part by the desire for insurance against
old-age unemployment, then families whose first three
offspring were male should have few if any additional
children. Those families whose first three offspring were
female should just be getting started. These inferences
were found to be correct.

Those family planners who had attributed irrationality to
the Indians had unknowingly expected them to commit
delayed suicide by limiting the size of their families.

Consider another example. At one time producers of gasoline advertised heavily in an effort to convince consumers
of the superiority of their respective products. There were
no significant performance differences between the different brands, but their producers assumed that they could
persuade consumers to the contrary and thereby induce
them to behave irrationally.

Subsequent research showed that the hundreds of millions of dollars spent on gasoline advertising were wasted;
it had virtually no effect on consumers. Behaving ration-

ally, they had no brand preferences. They bought gasoline at those service stations at which they believed the time required to get service was minimized. The oil company that sponsored this research was able to use these findings to increase its market share by locating, designing, and operating its stations to minimize service time. It also made reduced service time the theme of its advertising.

Corporate managers who think that consumers, employees, suppliers, competitors, or government officials are behaving irrationally should think twice and they should think differently the second time.

REFLECTIONS

Irrationality occurs, because people have different state of mind, different belief

35

Advertising: A Wonder or a Waste?

I've done a great deal of research on advertising that has convinced me that many agencies do a better job of selling themselves to their clients than of selling their clients' products or services to potential customers.

I find it difficult to understand why companies are willing to spend billions of dollars each year on advertising without any measure of its effectiveness. Advertising expenditures are based more on faith than fact. Agencies argue that the impact of advertising on sales cannot be measured because sales are affected by a large number of interacting variables and their effects can't be separated. *This is nonsense.* Modern experimental designs have been applied to "multivariate" situations for a long time and they have been used effectively to measure the results of advertising by several companies, including Anheuser-Busch.

Anheuser-Busch has learned by experiment that a number of assumptions commonly made about advertising are false.

First, increases in advertising do not always produce an increase in sales and, believe it or not, sometimes result in a decrease. The response to advertising is like the response to sales calls and most other types of stimulus. It takes a certain amount of advertising or sales calls to produce sales (Figure 9). This amount can be thought of as a *threshold*, beyond which sales increase with more advertising or calls up to a *saturation point* at which the customers cannot, or will not, buy more. Then, even with increased advertising or calls, sales remain relatively flat up to a *supersaturation point*. Beyond that customers are so annoyed

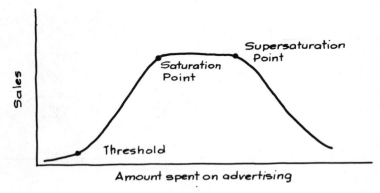

Figure 9.

by advertising or salesmen that they stop buying the products or services offered.

Companies that advertise beyond the supersaturation point, and there are many, can increase sales by reducing their advertising. This ought to be expected. Imagine what would happen to a product if *all* TV advertising were devoted to it or if a salesman decided to take up residence in a customer's establishment.

Although different populations respond differently to advertising, the shape of their response curves is the same. They have different heights and different locations on the horizontal axis (Figure 10); for example, heavy users of a product are generally the most responsive to advertising; moderate users, less so; and occasional users, least so. Then, if any population can be segmented into use-categories, a composite response curve can be obtained

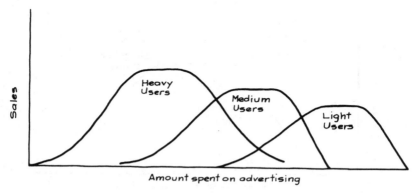

Figure 10.

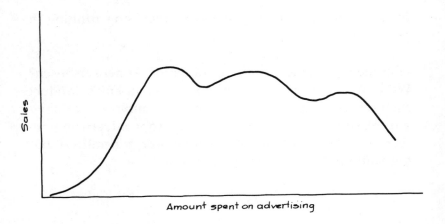

Figure 11.

(Figure 11). This composite curve can be used to maximize return from the investment in advertising.

It is also generally assumed that to be effective advertising must be continuous. It is clear, however, that if it is stopped for a day, no one notices. How long does advertising have to be discontinued before it is noticed and sales begin to fall? Most companies cannot answer this question. Anheuser-Busch can; it found that the length of time that one can be off a medium with no effect on sales is several times longer than most advertisers believe or that most agencies will allow them to believe. This finding made it possible for Anheuser-Busch to *pulse* advertising, to get the same effect on sales obtained by relatively continuous advertising but with a much smaller expenditure.

Furthermore, if a company uses several media, it can

phase its pulses on each to have advertising running in one medium at all times.

How generalizable are the findings of Anheuser-Busch? We don't know because only a few companies conduct such research, and many that do don't publish it for obvious reasons. The results obtained from advertising research by Anheuser-Busch should not be generalized, but the value obtained from it should be.*

REFLECTIONS

_____

_____

_____

_____

*For a more detailed description of the research done at Anheuser-Busch see Russell L. Ackoff, *The Art of Problem Solving*, Wiley, New York, 1978, Chapters 10 and 11.

36

Managing Interactions

A company is obviously a system. What is not so obvious is what this implies.

Many managers believe that if every part of a company, considered separately, is made to perform as well as possible, the company as a whole will perform as well as possible. Nothing could be further from the truth; for example, consider an automobile, a mechanical system. Suppose we ask a group of top automotive engineers to determine which make and model of car has the best carburetor and they choose one from a Buick. Then we ask them to do the same for the transmission and they select one from a Mercedes. Suppose we continue until we identify the best of each part needed to make an automobile. Then we ask the engineers to create an automobile by assembling those parts identified as the best. They would not succeed because the parts would not fit together. Even if they did, they wouldn't work well together.

The performance of any system, therefore of a company, is never equal to the sum of the performances of its parts taken separately. *It is the product of their interactions.*

For this reason effective managers do not focus on actions but on interactions. They coordinate and integrate the interactions of their subordinate units and individuals and those of their units as a whole with other parts of the organization. Effective managers do not manage the *actions* of the units and individuals reporting to them; they manage their *interactions* and allow units and individuals to manage their own actions. Employees at any level who cannot do their jobs without supervision are not fit for their jobs.

The management of interactions involves the *coordination and integration* of plans, policies, programs, projects, practices, and courses of action. This coordination and integration can be facilitated by providing each manager with a group—call it a board, committee, or whatever—that consists of (a) the manager, (b) the immediate superior, and (c) the immediate subordinates (see Figure 12). All managers except the one at the top and those at the bottom would serve on their own boards, their bosses', and their immediate subordinates'. In an organization with five or more levels, middle managers would have face-to-face interactions with five levels of management: their

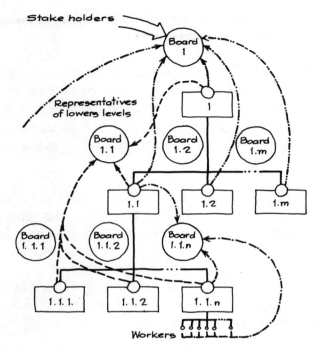

Figure 12.

own and two higher levels on their bosses' boards and two lower levels on their subordinates' boards.

Each board should have the responsibility for coordinating the actions of the level below it. Because subordinates are in the majority on the board coordinating them, they coordinate themselves with the help of two higher level managers. Except at the top and bottom of the organization, all managers participate in the coordination of (a) their subordinate units (on their own boards), (b) the units subordinate to their subordinate units (on their subordinates' boards), and (c) their units with others at the same level (on their superiors' boards).

Because all boards except the one at the top and those at the bottom consist of members who participate in two higher and two lower level boards, these boards can also integrate the plans, policies, programs, projects, practices, and actions of as many as five different levels of the organization.

It should be emphasized that boards manage the interactions of units, not their actions. They affect the actions of units or individuals only when the actions affect other units or individuals.

A number of organizations favor this system; for example, Anheuser-Busch, Clark Equipment Company, Tremec (in Mexico), the U.S. Naval Education and Training Command, and IECSA (in Argentina).

Managers in these organizations are frequently asked how they find the time to get their work done when they sit on as many as 10 boards. These boards meet no more than twice a month and seldom for longer than two hours. Therefore, even if a manager is active on 10 boards, no more than 40 hours a month are spent on them, or 25 percent of the time, *if* only a 40-hour week is worked. This leaves sufficient time for other activities, most of which are considerably less important than coordinating and integrating the units reporting to them and these units with others in the organization. Therefore, a more appropriate question would be: What do they do with the rest of their time?

REFLECTIONS

_____

_____

_____

_____

37

The Aesthetics of Work

Ancient Greek philosophers identified three ideals—*truth, the good, and beauty*—the pursuit of which they believed was necessary for progress and development. Modern man has added a fourth—*plenty* or *abundance*.

Science is dedicated to the pursuit of truth, and *technology*, to its application; *ethics and morality*, to the pursuit of the good; *aesthetics*, to beauty; and *economics*, to plenty.

These pursuits are relevant to management. Management science, business ethics and morality, and managerial economics are subjects that are familiar to managers. But what about the *aesthetics of work or management*? What in the world does that mean? It is not surprising that the answer to this question is not apparent because the aesthetician has been the "odd man out" for a very long time.

Although most people believe that we have made a great deal of scientific and economic progress and some believe that at least some ethical and moral progress has been made, few believe that there has been any aesthetic progress. We seem neither to produce more beauty nor to appreciate beauty more than preceding generations.

Aesthetics is the least understood aspect of progress and development. Little wonder, then, that most managers have no idea of its relevance to their work and that of others.

Aesthetics is related to two things: *recreation* and *creation*. Recreation is activity that refreshes one's mind and body, activity from which immediate satisfaction is derived, regardless of its outcome or consequences. It is *intrinsically* valuable; this means that its value lies in the *fun and enjoyment* we get out of it. To the extent that managing is fun and enjoyable, it has aesthetic value.

The creative aspect of aesthetics is reflected in the sense one can have of getting somewhere, of developing. It is this sense of progress that endows human activity with *extrinsic* value and makes it *meaningful*. Beauty *inspires*, produces visions of possible progress, and encourages the pursuit of these visions, whatever short-run sacrifices are required. Therefore, it *motivates* us to pursue development, to pursue progress. Recreation provides refreshing pauses in the pursuit of progress and makes the pursuit itself a satisfaction.

The currently growing concern with *quality of life*, in general and *work life* in particular is a matter of aesthetics. To improve the quality of life or work life is to increase the (recreational) satisfaction derived from what we do, whatever we do it for, and the (creative) satisfaction derived from making progress toward our ideals.

A few years ago the CEO of a very successful corporation asked me to look around his organization for any serious problems that were being overlooked. I spent several months traveling on reconnaissance. When I reported back to the CEO I told him there was one overriding problem that required attention: many of the company's employees, especially its managers, were not enjoying their work, thought it was unimportant, and had little sense of personal progress. As a result, their efficiency and effectiveness were deteriorating. The company was aesthetically deficient.

After some discussion of what might be done about it the CEO authorized an effort to improve the aesthetics of work. A participatively designed quality-of-work-life program for all employees was initiated and eventually succeeded.

Work that is neither fun nor meaningful is not worth doing well, no matter how much one is paid to do it.

REFLECTIONS

_____

_____

_____

_____

38

Friendship

Two of my academic friends once conducted an experiment built around a management game.* The game was played by teams of four graduate students selected at random, each assigned to a different role. One was made the chief executive officer and the others were assigned the responsibility for manufacturing, marketing, and finance. The game consisted of managing a simulated company in an effort to maximize a specified measure of performance. Before each team began its play the experimenters told its financial manager which decision rule would yield the best performance. However, the instructions were not to

*This is the same research described in Chapter 33 on "Fallibility."

reveal this rule to the other team members until they had played a while and a signal had been received from the experimenters. The financial manager was to pretend to have discovered the rule alone.

Very few of the teams that played this game accepted the optimal decision rule when the financial manager pretended to have discovered it. My friends, the experimenters, were surprised at this result. I suggested that they might increase acceptance of the solution by selecting students who were close friends to act as chief executive officer and financial manager.

The experiment was rerun according to my suggestion. The frequency of acceptance of the proposed solution increased significantly.

Friends are persons we know, like, and *trust*; we believe that they will act in ways that they perceive are in our best interests. Therefore, we are likely to take their advice more seriously than that of others.

When managers must make decisions quickly they are unlikely to accept the advice of anyone but a friend. They might accept the same advice from others if they had time to verify it for themselves. Without such verification they usually prefer to act on their own intuition than on nonfriendly or unfriendly advice.

It is for this reason that the most effective management

teams are those in which each member considers every other member to be a friend, regardless of rank.

The effectiveness of external consultants also depends critically on the personal relationships they establish with the managers to whom they report. In hundreds of research engagements at the university-based research center of which I am part, I have observed that the most successful projects are those in which the project leader and the responsible manager have become close friends. They interact socially as well as in the business context.

Friendship is most rapidly established by demonstrating an awareness and consideration of the personal welfare of others. Some people obviously have a greater capacity for friendship, but no one is completely lacking in it. It can be developed if a conscious effort is made to do so.

In most companies it is easier to form friendships among peers than across ranks. A great deal can be done, however, to facilitate the formation of "vertical" friendships. The fewer prerequisites and privileges used to differentiate ranks, the more task-oriented groups with members of different rank, and the more opportunity for informal nonbusiness interaction across ranks, the smaller the gap friendship has to bridge.

Any manager who cannot count an immediate superior, peers, immediate subordinates, and consultants as friends operates under a handicap that no amount of competence is likely to overcome.

REFLECTIONS

_____

_____

_____

_____

39

Respect

In my opinion a principal difference between excellent executives and others is the way that they use and are used by their subordinates. *They respect their subordinates and are respected by them.* They give their subordinates their heads but protect them from abuse or misuse by any higher authority or external source.

I once heard a CEO say something like this to a subordinate for whom he had a very high regard: "You consult me less than anyone else around here. That's OK as long as you continue to perform well. If you don't, I'll have your ass. Until then, I'll see to it you're free to do what you want and I'll give you any help you ask for and I can give. I could probably help you more if you kept me better informed. If you do, I promise not to intervene any more than I do now." The subordinate smiled, promised to keep him better informed, and thanked him. Mutual respect filled the room.

Another CEO once told me: "I can't do anything without good people. No organizational structure or culture, no leadership, no management style, and no amount of resources can make up for incompetent and uncommitted subordinates. The most important job of a CEO is to ensure the presence of competent and committed subordinates and to create an environment in which they can show their stuff."

Another executive, when approached by a subordinate for help in making a difficult decision, said, "I'm not going to make that decision for you. I won't even tell you what decision I would make if I were in your shoes. If I didn't think you could make the decision better than I can, you wouldn't be where you are. Now, if you want to discuss your problem because you think discussing it will help *you* make a better decision, fine. But if you want *me* to make it for you, forget it."

A first-class executive frequently seeks the advice of a subordinate. It is not always accepted, but when it isn't the rejection is always explained. When possible the subordinate is given a chance to rebut the rejection before action is taken.

Respect between superior and subordinate should be symmetrical. A highly valued subordinate was once confronted by his boss with a rumor that the subordinate was negotiating a move. The subordinate said, "It's not true. If I ever consider the possibility of moving, you'll be the first to know. On the other hand, if you ever think I ought to leave, I'd like to be the first to know." His boss agreed.

An internal candidate for a senior position in a company was asked by his prospective boss: "How do you think you can help me do my job better?" The candidate answered, "I can't answer that, but if you give me the job you'll be able to answer it after a while and I'll be able to tell you what you can do to help me to do my job better. It is my responsibility to find out how to use my subordinates, not how to be used by my boss. Few are the best judges of how they can serve others, but many are the best judges of how they can be served." He got the job and was first-rate.

A CEO once asked me to sit in on an interview of an external candidate for a vacant vice-presidency. After the candidate had entered and had been put at ease the CEO said, "It's a lot more important that this company be the right place for you than that you be the right person for this company. Therefore, I'd like you to interview me." The surprised candidate caught his breath and then did just that, with poise and intelligence. The CEO was incredibly frank in his replies to the candidate's questions, unashamed to reveal what he considered to be the weaknesses of the company and the detractions of the job. After the candidate had left, the CEO told me that both he and the candidate could learn a great deal more about the candidate's value to the company in such an interview than in the kind normally conducted. I agreed completely.

A good executive is a leader, not a commander, except in emergency situations. Above all else, an effective leader must have the *respect* of his or her subordinates and must respect them. Loyalty is not a substitute for respect, but a leader who is thought of as a *friend* by subordinates and in turn, thinks of them as friends, receives both.

REFLECTIONS

_____

_____

_____

_____

40

Consensus

When consensus—that is, *complete* agreement—is not reached by groups of managers faced with the need to make a decision, they often default or resort to majority rule.

The problem with less-than-unanimous majority decisions is that there is always a minority. Those in the minority are seldom as committed to implementation of the decision as are those in the majority. For this reason complete agreement is clearly desirable. But how can a consensus be reached when there is a difference of opinion? The answer lies in the fact that differences of opinion are more likely to rest on beliefs that involve matters of fact than on attitudes that involve matters of value; for example, supporters and opponents of capital punishment differ more on the effect they believe capital punishment has on the number of capital crimes committed than on the value they place on human life. Similarly, the current debate on abortion rests largely on a difference of belief as to when life begins but, again, not on the value of human life.

It is generally easier to dissolve differences of belief than differences of attitude. This can often be done by investigating the relevant facts in a way that is thought to be fair by all those concerned. Then, when the results are in, consensus can often be reached, even if it requires the majority to change its opinion; for example, in a large metal-producing company, executives could not decide whether to place maintenance under engineering or manufacturing. Their disagreement was based on differing beliefs about the impact of the alternatives on the effectiveness of maintenance. Because the company operated a number of similar plants, the executives reached a consensus on a test of the alternatives in different plants. When the results were in they reached complete agreement on the location of the function.

In a company in the food and beverage industry, agreement could not be reached on the appropriate amount to spend on advertising. However, the managers did agree on the design of an experiment in which different levels of advertising were used in a number of marketing areas. After several months this experiment enabled management to determine the effects of advertising on sales and to agree on the amount to be spent on it.

In some cases when consensus cannot be reached within the time available, no decision is made; current behavior is continued. This type of response can paralyze an organization. There is an alternative.

I once attended a corporate meeting at which nine different solutions to an organizational problem were presented, each prepared by a different team of managers. All the managers were present, but no agreement could be reached on which proposal was best and no proposal attracted majority support. They appeared to have reached an impasse. The chairman asked if I could suggest a way out of it. I proposed that the group make the following choice: either I would select one of the nine solutions at random or the organization would be left as it was. My suggestion was accepted and a vote was then taken. It was unanimous in favor of my making a random choice.

I didn't have to make the choice because the outcome of the vote suggested to the managers that they select one member from each team to form a group that would rework the solutions until they reached one on which all agreed. This was done and it succeeded.

It is frequently easier to get managers to agree that consensus is desirable than it is to obtain it. The additional time and effort required to reach consensus, however, is usually more than compensated for by the reduction in time and effort required to implement the decision it produces and the increase in the effectiveness of that implementation.

REFLECTIONS

_____

_____

_____

_____

41

Thinking, Reading, and Talking

Over the last 30 years I have spent as much time in corporate quarters as I have in the halls of ivy. The differences are striking. Although only a few aspects of academic life are worthy of corporate emulation, these few would do corporations a lot of good.

I have seldom seen a corporate manager sitting in his office deep in thought, reading something other than a business document, or discussing an idea rather than the problem at hand. These are activities that occupy much of an academic's time and a great deal of this time is fruitful.

Corporate cultures almost universally require managers to *look* busy, to appear to be *doing something* that is clearly business related. Thinking, reading books or journals, and discussing the ideas extracted from them is not generally considered to be "doing something." If managers engage in these activities, they must do so on "their own time." This is "not what they are paid to do."

Occasionally, of course, managers take part in management development programs in which they are exposed to and discuss ideas with their peers and purported experts; but it is not for this purpose that they are sent to these meetings. The expectation is that they will pick up some useful information, tools, or techniques—not ideas. If they were sent for ideas, they would be asked to share them with others when they returned. I have never heard of such a request being made.

These reflections were brought to mind a short time ago when I was having dinner with the CEO of a major corporation. During the meal, in which we did talk about ideas, he suddenly asked me the name of the last book I had read. I told him and we discussed it for a while. Then he asked me what book I had read before the last and we discussed that one also. When he made a third request I asked him why these questions. He told me that he did a great deal of reading "on his own time" but had no one to discuss it with at work. He said that his colleagues read little that was not immediately relevant to their work and that discussion of his reading *at work* would make him feel guilty; it would be perceived as unproductive.

Later I discussed this conversation with a number of his associates and learned that, in fact, they also did a good

deal of reading "on their own time" and felt it inappropriate to discuss at work. But they all said that they would
very much like to. I suggested that they organize periodic
"brown-bag lunches"—lunch-ins at which they hold such
discussions. They thought this was a good idea but no one
was willing to take the initiative.

When corporate executives visit me at the University I try
to have them take part in a bull session with students and
faculty. They invariably enjoy these sessions and tell me
how much they would like to participate in more of them.
My suggestion that they hold similar sessions at their
companies almost always evokes a shrug of the shoulders
and an expression of futility.

What a pity that so many managers indulge in such self-
deprivation and maintain a state of intellectual
undernourishment.

*The anti-intellectualism that pervades most corporations is
costly.* It makes it difficult for managers to keep up to date
with relevant ideas and to use them in their work. It also
deprives them of the even more important opportunity to
convert apparently irrelevant ideas into relevant ones.
Moreover, it denies them the fun and stimulation that can
be derived from "kicking ideas around," an activity that
enhances the quality as well as the productivity of work
life.

The search for and development of good ideas should be a
continuing preoccupation of managers. Such a preoccupation is not possible without thinking, reading, and

discussion. Without thought, there is little learning. Without reading, there is little to think about. Without discussion, it is difficult to distinguish between good and bad thinking.

REFLECTIONS

_____

_____

_____

_____

42

Learning

As everyone knows, we learn from our mistakes. But we have to know that we have made one before we can learn from it. Unfortunately, in the gap between making a decision and becoming aware of its results we often fail to recognize a mistake because our memory plays tricks on us; for example, at a meeting of corporate executives in which an inventory-control study was initiated, I suggested a pool on the change in the value of the inventory that would be brought about by the research. The suggestion was enthusiastically accepted. Each manager recorded his prediction, expressed as a percent change, on a 3 × 5 card, signed it, inserted it in an envelope with a 10 dollar bill, and sealed the envelope. The president gave the envelopes to the corporation's secretary for safekeeping.

The managers were kept well informed during the course of the study. When the results were reported to them it was decided to settle the pool. The president called the secretary and asked him to bring in the envelopes. The secretary did not appear. The president called again and told him to come at once. A very upset secretary appeared quickly and told the group that the envelopes could not be found. He could not explain their disappearance.

The managers were let down considerably. I suggested that all was not lost. I asked if they remembered their original estimates. They said they did. Then I asked each of them to record the original prediction on another card, sign it, and put up another 10 dollars.

When they had done so and I had collected their cards and money, I withdrew the original envelopes from my briefcase and proceeded to compare the first predictions with the "remembered" versions. There was significant variation. Needless to say, the ones remembered were much more accurate than the originals.

Our memories are far from passive. They modify their content to make us appear better to ourselves than we actually are. Therefore, when we make important decisions whose effects will not be known for some time, we should make a record of them that would contain

1. Their expected effects and when we expect them.

2. The assumptions on which our expectations are based.

3. The information used in making the decisions.

4. A description of how the decision was made and who participated in making it.

Decisions recorded in this way can be monitored not only to reveal our mistakes and the reasons for them but also to let us know, even before the results are in, when an underlying assumption is false. This often enables us to take action to prevent a mistake from being made.

A study made a number of years ago at the General Electric Company showed that managers who recorded the effects they expected of their decisions learned significantly more, and more rapidly, than those who did not.

The only ones who are incapable of learning are those who never make a mistake or are unaware of the mistakes they make.

REFLECTIONS

_____

_____

_____

_____

43

Understanding

Information, knowledge, and understanding are very different things. Information is contained in *descriptions:* answers to questions that begin with such words as "who," "when," "where," "which," and "how many." Knowledge is contained in *instructions:* answers to "how-to" questions. Understanding is contained in *explanations:* answers to "why" questions.

A wise man once said that an ounce of knowledge is worth at least a pound of information and an ounce of understanding is worth at least a pound of knowledge. Nevertheless, the time spent by most managers and management educators in acquiring and transmitting information, knowledge, and understanding is inversely related to their values.

Many explanations are nothing but restatements in different words of the facts to be explained; for example, in a study carried out for a multinational candy company my colleagues and I learned that per capita consumption of sugar in England was greater than it was in the United States. In an effort to find out why, I called a friend who was the marketing vice-president of a sugar company. I asked him if he was aware of the different consumption rates. He said he was. Then I asked if he could explain it. "Of course," he said. "The English like sugar more than we do." Because this was not what I was looking for, I asked, "How do you know they like it more than we do?" He replied, "They eat more of it, don't they?" This is like telling someone that a sleeping pill puts them to sleep because it's a soporific.

Misunderstanding, or even a lack of understanding, can get us into serious trouble. Consider a company that employed a large number of women as salaried inspectors of small items produced in the millions each year. The productivity of these women had decreased over the preceding five years and the plant manager decided to take corrective action. He thought he knew what made the women tick—money. As a result, he designed a piecework-compensation system that would require the women who wanted to maintain their earnings to inspect more items per day than they were doing at the time but fewer than they had five years earlier. If they handled as many as they once had, their earnings would increase significantly.

The plant manager proposed this scheme to the leaders of the union that represented the women. They rejected it summarily. The manager was furious and threatened to impose his scheme anyway. The union countered with the threat of a strike if he tried.

In desperation the manager turned to his research staff for help. Their investigation revealed that the women hated the plant manager because several years earlier he had refused to change their working hours. Most of them wanted to get out of work early enough to be home when their children returned from school. Moreover, they did *not* want to increase their earnings because this would put them in competition with their husbands for the role of family breadwinner. They saw their earnings as providing the "extras," not the necessities.

Armed with this understanding, the researchers designed a new compensation system in which a "fair day's work" was defined as the high average output of five years earlier. It was proposed that when the women had inspected this number of items they would be free to leave the plant. The women accepted this proposal with enthusiasm. Their rate of inspection increased dramatically and so did its quality.

The most important question a manager can ask when confronted with the unexpected or the undesirable begins with *why*.

REFLECTIONS

44

Managment Education

In my opinion, management education deserves all the criticism to which it has been subjected. In general it fails to prepare students adequately for the practice of management. But I think that most of the many changes proposed for improving it point in the wrong direction—to curricular changes. The major deficiencies in management education are not in *what* is taught but in *how* it is taught. The medium, the educational process, is more at fault than the messages transmitted by it; for example, a major part of management education is devoted to trying to solve problems given to students by teachers. As a result, students unconsciously come to believe that it is natural for problems to be *given* to them. In the real world, however, problems are seldom given; they must be *taken*. Nevertheless, students are neither taught nor learn how to take problems.

In management, problems usually have to be extracted from complex, unstructured, and messy situations. This can be learned only by practice, preferably under the guidance of someone who knows how. In learning to take problems, like learning to drive an automobile, instruction has little value without demonstration and practice.

Classroom work on case studies is intended to provide this practice but it cannot succeed. Cases are *distilled* descriptions of the real world. They reduce the complexity of reality and include only what those who prepare them consider to be relevant. Deciding what is relevant is a major part of taking problems.

Case studies do not present problems; they present *exercises*. The difference between problems and exercises is not widely appreciated, especially by educators; for example, a statistician once gave me the following so-called problem: "You reach into a bowl containing small black and white balls and pull out a handful. X percent of them are black; the others are white. Now, if you randomly draw an additional ball from the bowl, what is the probability it will be black?"

Instead of answering, I asked: "How do you know all the balls in the bowl are black or white?" He told me I was to assume it; it was *given*. But, I argued, I wanted to know how it was *taken;* if I knew this I could probably answer the question easily. He argued that such knowledge would spoil the problem. No, I said, it was already spoiled. It was an exercise, not a problem. *An exercise is a problem from which some of the information required to formulate it has been removed.*

Doesn't solving exercises help one to learn how to *solve* problems? It may, but solving problems is not the point; taking problems is, and one does not learn how by solving exercises. Moreover, learning how to solve exercises doesn't help much in learning how to solve problems. Teaching people how to box or play baseball with one arm tied behind their backs is not an effective way of teaching them how to box or play baseball with both arms free.

A student can best learn to identify, formulate, and solve problems by being exposed to and dealing with raw reality. Unfortunately, raw reality can't be brought into the classroom; but the classroom can be taken into the real world. Management education should require faculty and students to work together with responsible managers to identify, formulate, and solve problems that these managers actually face and this ought to be done in the environment in which they are faced. This would not only educate the students, it would also educate the faculty.

Faculty members need to learn how to take problems at least as much as their students. Teachers cannot teach what they do not know and especially what they do not know that they do not know.

REFLECTIONS

_____

_____

_____

_____

45

Town and Gown

Business schools do a much better job of educating their faculty than their students. Faculty members more than students are exposed to more business enterprises and more enterprises are exposed to them. Moreover, faculty members have many opportunities to absorb the learning of others, to reflect on, discuss, and try to understand their own learning and that of others, and to organize what they have learned to transmit to others. Managers have few of these opportunities. Much of faculty learning takes place in or is stimulated by discussion groups, organized or spontaneous. These groups are rare in business environments.

On the other hand, most managers learn more of relevance to their work on the job than they did at school. At work they absorb a great deal of information and some knowledge (skills) but gain little understanding. One can know a great deal about how to run an automobile or a business without understanding why they behave as they do. In contrast, business school faculties generally have more understanding and less knowledge of management and business than practicing managers.

Finally, students in business schools acquire little *relevant* knowledge or skills. To be sure, they learn all kinds of techniques, but most are not applicable to the problems they subsequently face on the job. They absorb little of the small amount of understanding that faculty members try to transmit because, as students, they generally lack the experiential base required for understanding. What business school students usually learn well are (1) a vocabulary that enables them to speak with authority about subjects they don't understand and (2) a set of principles that have demonstrated their ability to withstand large amounts of disconfirming evidence. Because of this, graduated students have to go through extensive *un*learning, as well as learning, before they become useful to their first employers.

How can the advantages of on-the-job education of managers and on-campus education of faculty members be combined and applied to managers, management educators, and students of management?

It might be done by organizing discussion groups at the workplace, by bringing together managers, educators, and students of management. These groups could be devoted to presentations and discussion of problems currently faced by managers, faculty members, and students and their efforts to solve them. Each would try to teach the others. *There are no more effective ways of learning than teaching and trying to solve problems with those who have them.*

Faculty members and students would benefit by sharing and reflecting on the managers' experiences. They would learn why many of the tools and techniques presented to students are not useful and they would become aware of the types of problem for which there is no relevant or effective body of knowledge. They might even succeed in getting some of their ideas tried and tested in practice.

Students could exercise their natural curiosity, skepticism, and cynicism by asking critical questions. (Even when they don't know the right answer to questions asked by others, they often know the right questions to ask them.) They would learn how to *take* problems, not merely solve those given to them. They would also learn how much more important it is to formulate a problem correctly than it is to find the best solution to one incorrectly formulated. A less than optimal solution to the right problem is more useful than the optimal solution to the wrong one.

And what might managers get out of these sessions? Some useful information, knowledge, and understanding, of course. But of greater importance, some ideas and the opportunity to think about and discuss them. They might even be moved to make thinking about and discussion of ideas fashionable in the work environment.

REFLECTIONS

_____

_____

_____

_____

46

The Fallacy of Forecasting

A great deal of the present is being wasted with efforts to forecast the future. In an environment that is rapidly changing and becoming more complex, our ability to predict the future necessarily decreases. Preparing for an inaccurately forecasted future is often worse than doing nothing. This is reflected in the old saying: "He who lives by the crystal ball ends up by eating glass."

Nevertheless, those who conceive of planning as preparing for a predicted future argue correctly that we benefit from forecasting the weather and preparing for it, although both are done imperfectly. True, but there is a significant difference between our relationship with the weather and a corporation's with what it forecasts in its planning.

Some believe that carrying an umbrella prevents rain and washing a car causes it. Nevertheless, *our preparations for the weather have absolutely no effect on it.* On the other hand, corporate planners forecast such things as the behavior of consumers, suppliers, competitors, and governments; and these things are affected by what corporations do. In fact, the principal purpose of planning is to affect them. Therefore, once a corporate plan that is based on a forecast has been prepared, the effects of that plan on what has been forecast should be taken into account by revising the initial forecast. But revising that forecast requires revision of the plan, which in turn requires another revision of the forecast, and so on *ad infinitum*. If all this were done, planning would take a course like that of the gilly-galoo bird, which flies in ever decreasing concentric circles until it disappears up its own anatomy.

Now, of course, this is not done. Predict-and-prepare planners treat the environment like the weather; they act as though it will be unaffected by their plans. Therefore, they try to control the effects of the environment on the organization planned for. The assumption that the environment is unaffected by what corporations do is sufficient to invalidate the forecasts used by planners and to make their preparations less effective than they desire.

Most forecasting is based on projections of the past into the future. Such extrapolations assume that the future is completely determined by the past. This assumption is sometimes approximately true for the *very near* future; but the more distant the future forecast, the more it depends on what will happen between now and then. This is even true for the weather.

Put another way: the more distant the future, the more it depends on decisions still to be made; therefore, the more subject it is to control. For this reason corporate planning should be directed toward trying to control the future, not the effects on a corporation of a future assumed to be out of its control. *This is exactly what we have done with the weather.*

Buildings are built to bring the weather under control. They eliminate the need to forecast the weather where we work and live. Even if we had perfect forecasts we would be better off working and living indoors than out.

Corporate planning should not consist of predicting and preparing for an uncontrolled future but of *designing a desirable future and finding or inventing ways of approximating it as closely as possible.*

REFLECTIONS

_____

_____

_____

47

Obstructions to Progress

The principal obstructions between an organization and what it most wants to be lie within the organization itself. Unfortunately, most managers and planners assume that these obstructions are imposed from without. Therefore, even if they succeed in removing or evading externally imposed obstructions, they often fail to get what they want because they neither remove nor evade the self-imposed constraints that are even more obstructive.

The principal obstruction to an organization's progress is usually the opinion of its managers and planners as to what is feasible; for example, in 1976 one of Mexico City's principal planners asked me to review and help him select the best of six alternative plans he had prepared to reduce traffic congestion in his city. After reviewing his plans I said that, in my opinion, none of them would work. He was shocked and wanted to know why. I explained that all of his plans were directed at increasing the supply of transportation enough to meet currently unsatisfied demand. He had neglected the fact that a new supply always creates new demand and this often exceeds the demand that was previously unsatisfied.

"Then you're saying there's no way to solve urban congestion problems," he said. "No," I replied, "they can be solved by reducing demand." This, he told me, was neither desirable nor possible in a democracy. I disagreed and he challenged me to tell him how it could be done.

I said "by moving a significant part of the federal government out of Mexico City." I pointed out that a large number of people in the city were employed by the federal government and that their emigration would reduce congestion by more than all six of his plans combined. Besides, there were good economic, ecological, and social reasons for moving the capital. "Of course," he said, "but you can't just up and move a nation's capital." I pointed out that the United States had done so twice. "But," he countered, "that was two hundred years ago." "What about Tanzania?" I asked. "It is contemplating a move of its capital right now." "But that," he said, "is in Africa."

He asked if I was aware that Mexico City had been the capital of the Aztec empire. I said I was, but that did not explain why the capital couldn't be moved. He then concluded that I probably never would understand because I was not a Mexican. There was no debating that point.

After an awkward pause in our conversation he asked if I could suggest another way by which demand could be reduced. I suggested that it be done by cutting the siesta, the two- to three-hour midday break, to no more than one hour. Midday trips between work and home were a significant part of the total number of trips taken and could be drastically curtailed. Moreover, I pointed out that today the siesta was seldom used for sleeping, although the bedroom was frequently involved. He then informed me that the siesta was an important part of Mexican culture and could not be changed. When I challenged him he said once again that I would not understand because I was not a Mexican.

Very shortly thereafter Lopez Portillo assumed the presidency of Mexico. In his inaugural address he announced his intention to disperse the federal government and decreed that all new federal buildings be built outside the city. He also announced a reduction in the midday break. In his first official act he had done two things that the city planner had told me were impossible.

The impossibility was obviously in the planner's mind, not his environment. This locus of obstructions to progress was recognized by the great American philosopher Pogo. On returning from a trip into the woods which he made "to hunt the enemy," he was asked by a friend if he had found them. He said he had. His friend asked who they were. Pogo replied, *"They is us."*

REFLECTIONS

_____

_____

_____

_____

48

Planning Backward

are → want to be

Most corporations plan forward, from now to then, a point in the future. Such *prospective* planning consists, first, of predicting the future to be prepared for and then preparing for it. The future prepared for is assumed to be out of the corporation's control, but its effects on the corporation are assumed to be at least partially controllable.

want to be → are

There is another type of planning—the *introspective*—that moves backward from what we want to be to what we are. It enables us to get much closer to what we want to be than planning forward from what we are. It does so because it expands our concept of what is feasible, our repertoire of potential courses of action.

188

In planning forward the feasibility of each possible course of action is usually evaluated separately. It is assumed that a course of action that appears to be infeasible when evaluated separately will continue to appear so when evaluated as part of a plan. This is not true. A plan is a set of interacting courses of action, *a system of actions*. A system always has properties that none of its parts has; for example, an airplane can fly us from one place to another but none of its parts can. Therefore, a plan can be feasible even though none of its parts considered separately appears to be so. Actions that appear to be infeasible when considered separately can appear feasible when considered as part of a system of actions. Planning backward enables us to consider each course of action as part of a system.

Introspective planning begins by assuming that the organization planned for disappeared last night. It no longer exists but its environment remains unchanged. The planners then design the organization with which they would most like to replace the one that "disappeared." This is called an *idealized redesign* because the only constraints imposed on it are, first, that it be technologically feasible—no science fiction—and, second, that the organization designed be capable of surviving in the current environment. However, *the design need not be one that can be realized now*. Therefore, practicality is irrelevant in making idealized design decisions. Yet, despite this, when such designs have been completed—and many have been—the responses to them have almost always been: "My God, we could realize most of it if we really tried."

An idealized redesign of a system reveals that the principal obstructions between an organization and what it most wants to be lie within the organization and that these barriers can be removed. This greatly expands our concept of what is feasible; for example, how feasible do the following proposals, considered separately, appear to be: that the capital of France be moved from Paris and that Paris be converted to an open self-governing city no longer subject to the government of France? Notwithstanding the apparent infeasibility of these proposals, the cabinet of France accepted them in the mid-1970s and has since taken steps toward their realization. How come?

In the early 1970s an idealized redesign of Paris was prepared by a large number of people both in and out of government. Although many political differences lay between them, they agreed that Paris ought to be *the capital of the world*. They didn't mean the capital of a world government because they didn't believe that such a government would come about in the foreseeable future. What they did mean was the principal location of the growing number of organizatons that deal with international affairs. Once this mission had been adopted, the redesigners saw the movement of France's capital from Paris and its conversion into an open city as not only feasible but *necessary*.

Planning backward consists of trying continuously to close the gap between what we ideally *want* to be *now* and what we *are*. We can get much closer to our ideals by working backward from them than by working forward from where we are. What follows is a case in point.

REFLECTIONS

_____

_____

_____

_____

49

The Clark–Volvo Joint Venture

On Wednesday, January 28, 1985, the Clark Equipment Corporation and AB Volvo of Sweden announced their intention to merge the Clark Michigan and Volvo BM divisions. This has since been done. Clark and Volvo have created one of the world's largest construction and mining equipment corporations. It is called VME, which are the initials of Volvo, Michigan, and Euclid. The story behind this joint venture merits a book. A brief commentary can hardly do it justice, but it is worth a try.

In 1983 Clark Michigan, which had not performed well during the recession, initiated a major effort to plan itself out of its mess. It began by formulating that mess: the fu-

ture that it would face if it continued its then current practices and policies and if its environment changed only in
expected ways. The future that was revealed by this analysis spelled doom for the division. In the time it had available it could neither generate nor acquire the resources required to redirect its future.

Rather than give up in despair, Clark Michigan's management designed without any constraints an ideal competitor of the two giants that dominate its industry—
Caterpillar and Komatsu. Again without constraints,
Clark Michigan's management selected those companies
in its industry that, with itself, would most closely approximate the ideal company it had designed. Three were
identified. These organizations, together with Clark
Michigan, resided in four different countries on three different continents.

Armed with this concept and design, Clark approached
Daimler-Benz, which owned the Euclid Truck Company,
and in almost record time arranged to acquire that company. Clark had already begun discussing a joint venture
with Volvo BM, the construction equipment division of
AB Volvo. Volvo displayed interest in the concept but had
a number of reservations. Clark responded by proposing
that a team be formed to address these reservations by
preparing a detailed design of the proposed joint venture
and evaluating its financial prospects.

Volvo agreed. A 10-man team, which consisted of the general managers of Clark Michigan and Volvo BM and their

production, marketing, financial, and engineering managers, was formed. This team began by producing a detailed idealized design of the Clark–Volvo joint venture. It drew up as nearly feasible an approximation of this design as it could. Finally, it made a financial comparison of the feasible design and the sum of two companies taken separately. This revealed that the proposal had potential financial advantages. The design team also felt that it had taken care of all of Volvo's reservations.

The feasible design was presented to the executives and boards of the two parent companies in the autumn of 1984. The design was approved and at the end of that year a commitment was made to implement it.

In addition to producing a creative and exciting design, the team members welded themselves into a homogeneous management group that overcame all the major cultural differences that were initially of great concern to both parties. By working closely for six months they even reached agreement on who should occupy each executive position in the new company.

With this cooperative design process the team anticipated and dealt with almost every problem that can arise in a joint venture. The process as well as its product enabled the two parent corporations to make their commitments with a degree of confidence that seldom characterizes such efforts.

REFLECTIONS

_____

_____

_____

_____

50

Responsiveness

Managers can reduce their dependence on forecasts by increasing their ability to respond rapidly and effectively to unexpected events; for example, when we take an automobile trip we don't arm ourselves with forecasts of road conditions, the number of drivers, how they will drive, and so on. Nevertheless, the likelihood of our reaching our destination depends critically on these things. We don't forecast them because we can respond quickly and effectively to most of what we might encounter. This means that we can avoid or minimize the undesirable effects.

We can increase our response capabilities by preparing for possible but unexpected events. When using an automobile, for example, we do not ordinarily expect a flat tire, but because we know one is possible we carry a spare. Our preparation is based on the *assumption* that a flat *can* occur, *not* on a *forecast* that one *will* occur. On the other hand, we don't carry a spare engine even though the one in our car might fail. If it did, we couldn't replace it by ourselves. We can prepare for such a failure better by joining an automobile club.

It would be foolish, of course, to plan for everything that can occur. We prepare only for those things that have a significant chance of occurring and with which we can deal without great cost or inconvenience.

Preparation for possibilities is called *contingency planning*, which consists of measures that can reduce the effects of conditions and events that would be costly or inconvenient if we did not anticipate them.

Because unexpected conditions and events occur frequently, corporate plans never work out exactly as expected. Therefore, they should be supplemented by contingency plans, preparation of which requires, first, identifying the possible events that can mess up normal plans; second, estimating the likelihood of each event and the cost and inconvenience of preparing for it; and, finally, selecting those events that justify attention and dealing with them.

Many of the unexpected events that spoil corporate plans are the result of unanticipated behavior of parties outside the corporation; for example, customers, suppliers, competitors, special interest groups, and government. By using *countermeasure* groups we can improve our anticipation of, and preparation for, the unexpected behavior of others.

A countermeasure group is a research team set up to act as though it were employed by a troublesome party; for example, a competitor, a supplier, or a customer. The task assigned to the team is to determine how that party, the "bad guy," can maximize obstructiveness. To facilitate this maximization the countermeasure team is provided with complete information about what the sponsoring corporation, the "good guy," intends to do.

Once the countermeasure team has determined how to obstruct the corporation, the corporation's planners take these obstructions into account and modify their initial plan appropriately. The countermeasure group then tackles the revised plan and tries to find ways of obstructing it. This process continues until the corporate planners believe they have covered all possible or likely contingencies adequately.

One corporation recently engaged in just such an exercise. It wanted to buy a plant put up for sale by one of its competitors. The firm interested in making the purchase was reasonably sure that another competitor would try to prevent the sale because it would be to that competitor's disadvantage. A countermeasure group, set up to represent the potentially obstructive competitor, determined what that competitor's first move should be if an offer to buy the plant were made by the sponsoring corporation. This corporation's management then prepared its response to that obstructive move. The countermeasure group returned to work. Four countermeasure cycles were completed before the countermeasure group could find no further way of blocking the purchase.

When the offer to buy was made, the obstructive competitor acted as though it were following the script prepared by the countermeasure team. Each of its moves had been correctly anticipated and was met with an effective response. The plant was successfully acquired.

The cost of preparing for critical events that do not occur is generally very small in comparison to the cost of being unprepared for those that do.

REFLECTIONS

_____

_____

_____

_____

51

Comprehensive, Coordinated, and Participative Planning

No group of corporate executives can prepare a comprehensive *corporate* plan with or without the aid of a planning staff. The most it can provide is an *executive* plan. The difference between these plans is best revealed by an example.

A Mexican brewer decided to give all of his employees an opportunity to participate in corporate planning. Those interested—and most employees were—received relevant instruction. They were then organized into small, homogeneous planning groups.

The top executives of the company formed one planning group but so did the janitors in the brewhouse. Obviously these two groups did not do the same thing. The executives considered such issues as diversification, acquisition, joint ventures, entry into new markets, facility requirements, and raising necessary capital. On the other hand, the janitors concerned themselves with redesigning the lavatories in the brewhouse, care of which occupied most of their time.

I have described this division of planning labor to many groups of executives. Invariably they smile. When they do I say, "This is cute, isn't it?" They nod in agreement. Then I ask: "But what has this to do with corporate planning?" Again they nod in agreement. I follow with an appeal for an honest answer to the following question: "What would happen to your corporation if the top executives were sent away for three months incommunicado and their offices were locked?" After some embarrassed tittering, the answer invariably given is: "Not much, if anything." (Some even suggest the possibility of improved corporate performance.) Then I follow with: "What would happen if the janitors were sent away for three months incommunicado and the lavatories were locked?" They get the point.

The point is not that the janitors are more important to the corporation than its executives but that the lavatories are as important a part of the corporation as its debt, product line, and markets. Therefore, a company's lavatories should be taken into account in its planning. If they are not considered, the planning is not comprehensive, however good it may be.

"But," some respond, "the lavatories will be taken care of

even if not planned for. So why include them in the plan?" The answer lies in the *way* they will be taken care of and in how those who take care of them will feel about their work. This is shown in what happened to the initial plan prepared by the janitors in the brewhouse. The people who did the brewing also prepared a plan. It included a redesign of the brewhouse. When they had completed their revision they and the janitors met to study the two plans. It was immediately apparent to both groups that they did not mesh: the brewhouse workers had neglected the lavatories and the changes suggested by the janitors interfered with the brewing process. Therefore, a combined group was formed to produce a coordinated plan for producing beer and for getting rid of it.

A similar process took place on the packaging line. When an integrated plan for this line was completed the brewhouse and packaging groups were brought together and shown both plans. Again they did not mesh. A joint effort subsequently succeeded.

This process continued across the lowest level of the organization and was duplicated at every other level. At the same time the planning staff of the corporation reviewed each plan as it was produced and called it to the attention of any other group, at whatever level of the organizaton, to which it was relevant. This led to meshing plans produced at different as well as at the same levels.

As a result of this process employees throughout the corporation came to *understand* how their activities affected and were affected by other corporate activities and, most important, *how they affected the overall performance of the corporation*. This understanding led to a radical transformation: each unit began to plan and operate to optimize the performance of the corporation as a whole rather than just its own. The improvement in corporate performance brought about by the reorientation of its parts is the principal benefit to be derived from corporate planning. *This benefit cannot be realized unless the planning is comprehensive, coordinated, and participative.*

REFLECTIONS

_____

_____

_____

_____

52

Continuous Planning

The planning pie can be sliced in many different ways, one of which consists of dividing it into six parts or phases.

1. *Setting up:* formulating the situation the organization is in by identifying the threats and opportunities it faces, the ways in which they interact, and the obstructions that constrain what can be done about them. This, I believe, is best done by projecting the future the organization would have *if* it were to continue on its present course and *if* its environment were to change only in expected ways. This *reference projection* is a picture of the "future that the organiza-

tion is in." It is *not* a forecast of the organization's future because it is based on two assumptions ("ifs") known to be false. If the organization intended to continue on its present course, it would not be planning, and no organization expects its environment to change only in expected ways. Nevertheless, a reference projection is useful because it reveals how and why the organization's performance would deteriorate if it were to continue on its current path.

2. *Ends planning:* designing an ideally desirable present and determining the differences between this present and the future revealed by the reference projection. These differences constitute the gaps that the remainder of the planning process should attempt to close or reduce.

3. *Means planning:* selecting or inventing the means by which efforts will be made to close or reduce the gaps. Means assume such varied forms as courses of action, practices, projects, programs, and policies.

4. *Resource planning:* estimating how much of each type of resource will be required by the means selected, when they will be required, and how much will be available; determining how the deficiencies revealed will be removed by acquisition or generation of additional resources and how the excesses revealed will be used or disposed of. Five types of resource should be taken into account: people; facilities and equipment; materials, energy, and services; money; and information.

5. *Design of implementation:* scheduling and assigning responsibility for the things to be done.

6. *Design of controls:* setting up procedures for (a) determining whether they are being done as expected and, once done, whether they are producing the intended effects, and (b) taking corrective action when implementation or its effects deviate from expectations.

Resource planning and controlling the implementation and effects of a plan make it necessary for planning to be *continuous*, not an off-again–on-again process.

The resources required by the means selected in the planning process seldom, if ever, are equal to the amount needed. In turn, demands are for sequential revisions of ends, means, and resource plans; for example, in a plan produced by a company in the consumer products industry the planners proposed building a new plant that would be about twice the size of the largest plant of its type that had ever been built. Because of the large investment involved, board approval was required. The board accepted the need for the large plant but was unwilling to incur increased debt to build it. The planners were instructed to try to generate the required capital internally.

Fortunately the planners found a way to reallocate production to the company's existing plants that would reduce costs enough to provide the required capital and more. When they returned to the board with this result construction of the new plant was approved. However, they were asked how they intended to use the excess capital that would be generated. The planners suggested diversification. The board agreed but asked what kind of diversification. The planners replied that plans had not yet been prepared. The board asked them to do so and submit their results.

Three possible diversification plans were developed, each based on a different type of product or service. When these plans were presented to the board it decided it wanted to pursue all three. Because enough capital would be available to implement only one of the plans, the planners were sent back to find ways of generating the capital required to implement the others.

This continuous planning cycle began about 20 years ago. It is still going on.

Furthermore, because plans are never implemented exactly as expected and the effects of implemented plans always deviate from expectations, effective control requires that plans be modified almost continuously.

To be effective, planning cannot be a sometime thing, off-again–on-again. It must go on all the time. The output of effective planning is no more a discrete plan than the output of producing a motion picture is a still photograph clipped from it. It is an ever-changing plan, one that reflects the continuous learning and adaptation of those who prepare it.

REFLECTIONS

_____

_____

_____

_____